From a Country Boy's View

Clifton, Virginia - the 1950's

by

Michael (Mike) Foley, Sr.

Bloomington, IN  Milton Keynes, UK

authorHOUSE™

AuthorHouse™
1663 Liberty Drive, Suite 200
Bloomington, IN 47403
www.authorhouse.com
Phone: 1-800-839-8640

AuthorHouse™ UK Ltd.
500 Avebury Boulevard
Central Milton Keynes, MK9 2BE
www.authorhouse.co.uk
Phone: 08001974150

First published by AuthorHouse 7/19/2006

ISBN: 1-4259-3006-9 (sc)
ISBN: 1-4259-3007-7 (dj)

Printed in the United States of America
Bloomington, Indiana

This book is printed on acid-free paper.

Table of Contents

Dedication

To Mom and Dad, Karen, Kevin, Chip, Duffy,
Mr. Porter and our unofficial brother Jon

Mike Foley - First grade
Clifton Elementary

Prologue

Anybody who reads this book has got to realize it was a lot of fun growing up on a farm in the 1950's and early 60's. I have done the very best I could to portray life in and around Clifton, Virginia and what it was like growing up on a farm at that time. My stories are as accurate as memory can provide and have not been fabricated even a smidgen. Although an adult, I have tried to tell my stories through the eyes of the child who lived them – My stories are true - and as real as a Blue Jay hoggin' a bird feeder. Kids today will probably figure that I made this stuff up. I didn't! To them, all I can say is: "Get away from your video games and T.V. set for a day or two and go outside and do something fun with your life".

The 1950's and early 60's were a time in history when kids could do almost anything they wanted to do without the adverse influence of the modern media. To me, Andy of Mayberry was real and was both the mentor and reflection of the time.

This book strives to regress from the computerized fast-paced life of the twenty first century to a serene time of yesteryear; a time wherein infinite adventure, close family ties, understanding, wisdom and love prevailed. From a Country Boy's View is a simple story of adolescence and the subtle tale of growth, learning and appreciation.

If I am ever blessed with Grandchildren, I hope they have something to tell their kids about their youth - other than sleeping in half the day, playing video games in their air conditioned house – and then driving their parent's car to the mall - wasting the rest of the day. There's a big difference between living and existing....

My advice to kids today: "Life's short – go live it"!

December 31, 2005

The Farm

As with any young and adventurous 7 or 8 year old, school days had a strange similarity to that old saying, "A Watched Pot Never Boils", but they did end as I recall. By late afternoon when the school day was over - we did finally get home. I say "Finally", because Mr. Doak, the school bus driver, never went over about 20 miles an hour at any given time, thus earnin' him the nickname "Slow Poke Doak" for obvious reasons. Not only was the 'round trip an hour or so each way but he drove that old dilapidated bus # 50 at a snail's pace. Slow Poke Doak in appearance had a likin' to Abe Lincoln with about as much personality as a toad frog. The guy just never understood how important my gettin' home was in an attempt to salvage what was left of an otherwise wasted day. I never had too much use for the guy, but tolerated things as they were because there wasn't anything I could do about 'um anyway. When I finally got home I would throw my school stuff down on the kitchen table and head out somewhere fixin' to do somethin', with more of an idea or hunch than an actual plan. Mom never asked many questions or fretted much about where I was goin' or what I intended to do. She knew I had some grand plan that couldn't wait and that I'd either be on foot or on horseback so I couldn't go more than a mile or so. She 'most always gave me credit for havin' good sense. The credit for good sense part just shows how wrong some Moms can be, from time to time.

Mr. Porter knew just about everything. He served as my mentor and part time Dad durin' the week when my own Dad was bustin' his hump to make ends meet for the family. What little Mr. Porter didn't know, he made up with incredible jaw-droppin', bug-eyed, edge-of-the-chair-sittin' believability to a young boy. I hadn't been lucky enough in those days to own a bicycle, due to the fact that we lived quite modestly while Dad was strugglin' to make him a career. The Porters' house was up the road and 'round the bend no more than about five minutes walkin' or about a minute and a half on the run. After school on cold and rainy November afternoons I headed over to see him as I did 'most every other day of the year anyway. I very seldom ever made it past the kitchen on a visit, due to the fact that that's where country people spend most of their time. Mr. Porter was a large man by little boy standards, half Cherokee Indian with white receding hair, a chiseled nose and a smile of genuine sincerity. He had large and sinewy hands and a peg leg. His right leg had been amputated just below the knee durin' World War I and the war was about the only thing he never talked about too much. I spent a lot of time studyin' his home-made fake leg when I figured he wasn't lookin'. Mr. Porter had made the thing in the open-ended shed beside his house from a single piece of wood, using no more than country creativity, an antique draw knife and an old wooden vise which I'm sure was home-made too. The contraption looked store bought but it and hardly anything else he owned came out of the Sears & Roebuck catalogue or any other store for that matter! It was a beautiful piece of old-time craftsmanship with a padded "U" perfectly shaped for his knee when the six or so inches of his lower leg was bent backward. The upper portion strapped to his thigh with leather bindin's while the lower portion tapered to about the size of a square silver dollar. He put a piece of old car tire on the square pegged bottom, kinda' like the sole of your shoe and the device fit him perfectly. I don't recollect Mr. Porter ever complainin' about anything even his bum leg.

The house had no heatin' system and the flat top, four burner wood stove in the kitchen served as a dandy source for warmth and fixin' dinner. The livin' room was the only other room in the house short of the upstairs and had an upright wood stove which serviced the rest of the house in winter. His house was like most of the old rural farmhouses back then, which meant - if you had to relieve yourself - it was - behind the shed and over the hill to the outhouse. Most modern folks these days can't relate to a real genuine outhouse and about all they've ever seen is a portable Johnnie-On-the-Spot. I always thought an old time outhouse was pretty cool, but never could quite grasp the concept of how one size wooden bench-like seat somehow fit everybody. The other thing I never understood, nor which I ever asked about, was just why there were always two sittin' spots in those little tiny things. Seemed to me that if somebody had to do some sittin', I ain't sure I'd want any part of sittin 'long side of 'um while they was sittin'. I've heard talk about usin' the old Sears catalogue pages and corn cobs for toilet paper but I think that went on a little further back before my time. I do know one thing for sure, had I ever asked such questions, Mr. Porter would have known the answers. I'd a bet ya fifteen cents to a plugged nickel that the Porter's outhouse was more of his handiwork. I'm gunna' tell ya what - the guy had an eye for detail too. There was a perfect "Quarter Moon" carvin' on the wood hinged door. Those old outhouses served the purpose just fine - 'though maybe a little inconvenient in the wintertime.

Mr. Porter could tell me a yarn on any given subject. He told me all about the time when he was in Africa and shot a bull elephant right in the heart. And then there was the time in Alaska when he shot a chargin' Kodiak bear right between the eyes and dropped him in his tracks, plumb dead. He also told me, "Dogs don't bite". He told me when ya come on to an ornery one, just stand your ground, look 'um in the eye and start talkin'. Said they'd back down every time. I had an occasion to try that bit of wisdom one time and ended up climbin' a tree. When I told him about the situation, he said it didn't work 'cause I wasn't holdin' my mouth right. Well, I've heard that expression a few times since and I think it's just an old fashion country way of bypassin' the subject. By and large the dog trick does work most of the time but then, sometimes it all depends on the dog.

Out in the work shed beside Mr. Porter's house, leanin' against a wall was the coolest shillelagh a boy had ever seen. The club was about four feet long and made of a single piece of hickory. The shaft was just the size at the end for getting your hands around real good like a baseball bat and enlarged a trifle as it ended at a perfect club bottom. Kinda' looked like a one wood in a golf club set but enlarged considerably in circumference. The bark was still on the whole thing and had been shined up a bit to look old and worn. About the time he detected I took a shine to that thing, Mr. Porter started tellin' me its history and where it came from. Told me how the shillelagh had belonged to a guy named Shauness O'Murphy, in Ireland back in the 1600's. He claimed that Shauness was the roughest, toughest man that ever lived on the Emerald Isle. His physical description of the guy was with a great amount of detail, like everything he described, and the guy had the physical likin' to Paul Bunyon. My young minds keen eye was pegged on Shauness, as though he was standin' right there in the shed. There wasn't much I wouldn't a done to be the proud owner of that shillelagh. I could tell Mr. Porter wasn't much on partin' with the thing, and every time I went to see him the stories kept gettin' bigger and better. He told me how every time Ireland went to war with Scotland, England or even Communist Russia, Shauness was at the head of the pack – no guns, no knives – just that club. Mr. Porter claimed he killed many a bad guy with that thing in defense of Old Ireland. As the stories got better and better, Mr. Porter picked up real quick on my interest and infatuation. The more he piled it on - the more I ate it up. I let him know how much I'd like to have that thing and the more I let him know, the better the stories got and the less he was apt to part with it. Got down-right flusteratin' at times!

Caught him at a weak moment one day and he told me I could have that doggone thing. I must'a been dreamin', that just couldn't be happenin'. Thought I was hallucinatin' - like he'd hit me up side the head with it or somethin'. Me, with the Shillelagh, that the famous Shauness O'Murphy once defended Ireland with was too good to be true – but it was true. I didn't play none too hard to get – I took it! That shillelagh went with me every trip to the woods or creek and 'most everywhere I went. I knew as long as I had it I was safe, after all, Mr. O'Murphy took on armies and bad guys and I didn't figure there was any of either within at least 50 miles.

It was February 1, 1951 right on the dot when my family moved from Falls Church, a little ol' town in the shadows of Washington, D.C. to the most remote area of rural Fairfax county, Virginia. I remember that real good because the next day was "Groundhog Day" and that particular Groundhog's Day was my third birthday. I recall the day as vividly as a mornin' sunrise because mom and dad got two hogs for the farm and claimed they were my birthday present. I later figured the birthday present thing was a convenient excuse for gettin' the hogs and not a well thought out birthday gift. Supportin' that notion - they named one Hetty and the other Anna. Coincidentally, those two names were the same first names of my two Grandmas! I never heard before or since about anybody gettin' two hogs for their birthday. Either way, supposedly they belonged to me and it was two more hogs than I'd ever owned before. We named another sow hog "Messy Bessy" due to the way she wallered in the mud. A couple of years later she gave birth to eight little piglets. One day she was just layin' there in the foot deep mud of the pigpen with her piglets at the milk bar and decided to roll over. We went from eleven pigs back down to three about that quick.

The old house in Falls Church was a tiny little thing, probably no more than 800 square feet total counting the back porch and sat on around a quarter of an acre - in a subdivision to boot. The new wooden farmhouse (New to us) was built in 1921 and the only reason that I knew that was 'cause someone had scratched 1921 into the concrete floor on the screened in porch. Looked to me like they most likely done it when the concrete was still wet, so I just figured 1921 for the whole thing. The new house seemed huge by comparison with two stories and an endless number of hidin' places for a little boy. Everything and every day brought somethin' new to a three year old and there was no concept of movin' from a congested area (By 1951 standards) to a farm in the middle of nowhere. Took me a while to figure that one out. In those days the county roads were dirt roads as opposed to paved and we didn't even have telephone service. Thinkin' back though, I don't remember any telephones at the old house either. When they did finally bring phone service out to the boon-docks, we had one of those black old rotary dial phones and the service was a party line. The way a party line worked was that the phone company would give one number (Ours was BR 88551) to three or four different families in the same general vicinity. When the phone rang often times there would be several different people sayin': "Hello" at the same time. When ya finally figured out who it was for, you'd always heard a few rattlin' hang-ups and the person who it was for just went on with the conversation. The lousy thing about a party line was that if you were on the phone and a neighbor wanted to use it, they just kept pickin' it up to see if you were still there. If so, they'd hang it up with the disgustin' sound of the talkin' part of the phone hittin' on the hook. After doin' that at a rate of about once a minute the message was pretty clear and you were better off to just hang the damn thing up wait a minute or two and return the favor. A party line seems inconceivable today, but by the standards of the early fifties and never havin' had a real telephone, we were in "High Cotton".

'Long about 1955 we had that farm lookin' pretty good. Dad got himself an old Ford tractor and drove the thing around like there was no tomorrow. I do believe he fantasized bein' a Roman Emperor or somethin' – surveyin' his domain when ridin' through the fields. There wasn't no other logical explanation. In time he came across a pretty decent sized two wheeled trailer that hooked right up to the tow ball on the back of the tractor. There wasn't no such thing as trash service back in those days so you had to get rid of your own, anyway ya could. What we did was take the bottles and cans out and burn the rest in a homemade incinerator. When it came to table scraps and the stuff that generally starts stinkin' in time, well, that's what the "Slop" in sloppin' the hogs was all about. We seemed to have a way of gettin' rid of about anything back in those days without makin' a mess. Every now and then we'd take the unburnable stuff to the dump. The dump wasn't any county landfill or anything like that - it was our own home made dump on our own property. Dad designated a spot back in the woods on the way to Marshall and Nelly's house, (Talk about country folks, just wait 'til I get to that part of the story) and that's where we got rid of the real junk. Plastic trash bags hadn't been invented yet so we just piled the stuff anyway we could on the trailer and headed on back. Goin' to the dump was a real thrill. Dad was always the designated driver as any of the rest of us kids were too little to drive the tractor. Didn't really make any difference though whether we could drive it or not – Dad was gunna' to be the driver. I think the ol' tractor gave Dad a sense of power or somethin' of the like, 'cause he had a strange fascination with it. Ownership, perhaps - kinda' like your dog. Your dog is your dog, and there ain't no two ways about it!

There wasn't a whole lot to do on the farm other than to think up somethin' to do and just go do it, so a trip to the dump was country boy fun. Dad would fire up the tractor and we kids jumped on any way we could, hangin' on for dear life at times, 'cause it was so much more fun to be ridin' somewhere than walkin'. It was usually three of us at a clip not countin' Dad and the trip was about a half mile along the dirt road separatin' two fields and on into the woods. The road extended beyond the dump about a mile, give or take, and ended at a mighty nice fishin' cove along Bull Run river about ten miles downstream from the Manassas battlefield. My brother Chip and I had eagle eyes when we were kids and often times spied an Indian arrowhead in the plowed field along the way. We'd jump off the tractor grab the artifact and jump back on without Dad havin' to stop or in a lot of cases without his even knowin' that we done jumped off and then back on.

When we got to the dump the real fun began. Chip and I specialized in the disposin' of the bottles. We'd either throw them against something so as to smash 'um or one of us would throw one up in the air and the other would try to bust it in mid air with another bottle. That was our primitive prelude to later shootin' clay pigeons, or least ways learnin' how to lead the target. It always amazed me at how many kill shots we had at the dump. If we missed, a good bottle would be retrieved for a second or third throwin' 'til we busted it into smithereens. There was a lot of good junk back there at the dump and now and then we'd retrieve somethin' to take back home. Mom and Dad didn't think none too much of us bringin' stuff back to the house that they'd done thrown away once.

The one bad thing about the dump was that 'most everything was biodegradable. Many years after leavin' the farm I took my first wife, Pat to see where I had grown up. Back in the 50's, Styrofoam, plastic bags and the like hadn't been invented yet. The bottles were long gone into tiny pieces and the tin cans had long since rusted away. I found where the dump had been but the years had completely rotted everything away. All of those fun times were now only a memory – but a damn good one.

The Foley family 1950 - from left to right:
Dad with Duffy, Kevin, Karen, Chip, Me and Mom.

Mom and Mr. Porter

Dad, Karen, Chip, Kevin & Me

Falls Church, Virginia - summer of 1950
Karen, Me, Kevin, Dad and Chip

Easter Sunday 1953
Kevin, Chip, Karen & Me

Big kids and hollyhock
Karen, Chip, Kevin (Check out the mini-skirt) & Me

House, driveway and front of house summer 1952

Corncrib left, tool shed right January 1957

Kevin, Chip, Karen and Me - summer 1952

Karen with her new calf, Abigail

Me, Kevin, Karen and Chip with the redbone pups

Mom with Maggie on left and Duffy on the right

Mom with Smokey

Mom and Dad Christmas Day 1952

The farmhouse

Clifton, Virginia

I don't guess too many people have ever heard of Clifton, Virginia. Least ways that's how it was when I lived there. Times do change though and what was, may no longer be, and what is might not have been at all and vice versa or something like that. Our farm was about three miles out of town and our mailin' address was Route 1 Box 214 Clifton so I guess we were residents. On the map, if they even showed it at all, the town was about 25 miles southwest of Washington D.C., which was the capitol of the United States at the time – and still is.

Mom used to refer to the town as "The Village" and I suppose it was, in fact, more of a village than a town. There were a total of five roads leadin' to Clifton and all five were posted with Corporate Limits signs, so I guess whether anyone had ever heard of it or not, the place did exist and that made it official. The truth of the matter is - five roads were leadin' into town but one of 'um just kept on goin' with a Corporate Limit sign on both ends - so it all depended on which way you were headin' as to how you counted the roads.

Clifton was a quaint little country town with a main street, two general stores, a post office, a volunteer fire department, two churches, a two-rail train track, an elementary school and a one man barber shop. That was it. Ambler's Store closed down in the mid 50's which left only one. The main street was about as long as the barbed wire fence on our back field which made it a couple of hundred yards give or take. There was one boarded up store and one boarded up hotel, from who knows when, and two of about ten houses were likewise. Nothin' fancy 'bout the place just a little ol' country town where everybody seemed to be some kin to everybody else. The old hotel was a two-story structure from the Victorian era and as rumor had it John Singleton Mosby, "The Gray Ghost" of the Confederate Army used to stay there, from time to time, after the Civil War. Don't know that to be fact but that's what the old timers used to say. I reckon that's another one of those questions I should have asked Mr. Porter but never got around to. The population of Clifton wasn't all that many due to the fact that most of the folks lived on farms. The elementary school was serviced by two school buses, which went in two different directions. Each serviced about 20 miles of country roads gatherin' up the hand full of students at the school. There was an old man by the name of Mr. Padget who dressed in a navy blue police uniform, hat, badges and all, and manned the railroad crossing every single mornin' and afternoon of the school year. He never missed a day. Old man Padget was a bifocaled, pot-bellied older guy who actually had a glass eye and didn't mind taking it out every now and again. Rumor had it he was a retired D.C. cop and that's most likely where the uniform came from. There wasn't no paycheck for doin' what he done, he was just kinda' weird about the whole thing and didn't mind doin' it. His mission was simply to make sure the walkers (Kids from town) and the bus made it across the train tracks safely. He made a big "To-Do" when either the kids or the bus were about to cross the tracks. He'd hold up his hand in a demandin' sort of way and bid them halt. He then looked both ways down the track and when all seemed clear, he'd wave the passers-by forward. We all laughed at him behind his back 'cause of three things. First of all, us kids figured he was half nuts, second the trains never ran in either the early mornin's or afternoons and third there was a trip gauge a mile or so down the track that set off the blinkin' alarm and lowered the cross bars. Mr. Padget's heart was in the right place - it's just that his timin' in life was off a little. His inspiration may have been our neighbor, Mrs. Clifford whose car once stalled on a track and got hit by a train. The accident wasn't fatal but her hair turned white over night. I just bet cha' he went to his grave knowin' that he had saved some kid's life - and maybe did. Between startin' each day with Mr. Padget and Slow Poke Doak, I guess we really did need to get to school and associate with the stupid teachers who did sometimes make sense!

The Clifton General Store was originally an old garage that fixed up broken down cars and looked more like a blacksmith shop than a repair place. Later it was bought and fixed up lookin' much as the current general store. It was then owned and run by Mr. and Mrs. Price, an elderly couple and as nice as the day is long. In the 50's there was a two-cent deposit charged on all sodas. Sodas didn't come in cans back then, only bottles. What that meant was after you drank the coke, or whatever, you could take the empty bottle back to the store for a two-cent refund or just throw 'um out the car window like a lot of folks did. I couldn't any more afford a store bought coke than I could afford a Sputnik, so I picked up empties along the road and cashed the bottles in for the deposit. Sometimes I had to cover two miles of road to gather a half dozen bottles (I had a use for litter-bugs back then). When I lined 'um up and multiplied 'um out by two, I felt rich. Twelve cents equated to twelve one-cent fireballs. That was about as close to "Hog Heaven" as I could get in those days!

There was an old dilapidated house just up the road from the driveway to Clifton Elementary. The guy that lived there was an elderly black man by the name of Eli Stokes. Aunt Doris called him "Old Dirty Shirt" and if'n ya ever seen him, it didn't take much imagination to figure why. Ol' Eli's sole means of transportation was a buckboard wagon and an old mule. You'd see him ridin' around on both sides of town – never seemed to have anything in the buckboard – just ridin'. Eli never had much to say and when he did, ya couldn't hardly understand him anyway. Life was a slow pace back in the 50's and he was a slow pacer.

On the way out of town like you were going toward the Kincheloe farm there was a pretty steep hill headin' up. At the base of the hill on the right side where Chestnut Street hooked up with the main street was an old church called the Primitive Baptist Church. Rumor had it that that church was the oldest church in the whole state of Virginia. The church was supposedly built by the negro slaves prior to the civil war and was for negro people only. Since there weren't too many negroes around Clifton in the 50's they'd come from as far away as Washington, D.C. to worship there on Sundays. Up the road a hop, skip and a jump on the left side is where Jesse and Nelly Fairfax raised four kids – David, Robert, Earl and little sister Kay. It was actually Nelly that done most of the raisin' if the truth be known. The Fairfax boys were among the coolest kids in town. I never really knew Kay 'cause she was so much younger than all the rest.

Headin' on up the hill on the right side was a small building they called The Odd Follows Hall. Never really knew too much about that place or what went on there so I'll just move a little further on up the hill. The next thing on the right was another negro church called the Second Baptist Church. That was a little ol' thing and I ain't sure much went on there. At the top of the hill was where the Selby family lived. There were three kids, Harry, Charles and Margaret. Harry was the oldest and I never got to know him very good but Margaret was my age and we were in the same grade in school. Charles was the middle kid and a little on the wild side. Some people called him "Charlie Horse". The reason for that was 'cause he had an ol' sway back nag he used to ride up and down the main street of Clifton. He'd gallop that poor old dilapidated thing up and down the main street with sometimes as many as three other kids on the horses back.

On the road parallel to the train tracks goin' toward Fairfax Station was the Clifton Volunteer Fire Department. They had some shin-digs at that joint – Saturday night dances, community functions and all kinds of stuff. Matter of fact, that's where the Clifton Boy Scout troop met once a week. Pete Petersen, the father of Donny, David, Doug and Jimmy started that thing up and did a really good job.

He was dog-gone strict on us boys when it came to knowin' and practicin' the scout motto, scout oath, scout laws and how to tie about every knot ever tied in the whole wide world. When test takin' time came around to become a tenderfoot in rank, there weren't no gimmies – either you passed or failed. We camped out as a group a few times over on the Prince William county side of Bull Run. Bein' a Boy Scout was a really good and fun time in my life and I'm proud to say I was one.

The people next door to us were the Lewises. They didn't have any runnin' water in their house but did have a well not far from the back porch. I thought it was so cool when Mrs. Lewis would ask me to draw a bucket of water for her from the well and I did it without bein' asked twice. That was some mighty good drinkin' water too, I might add. The way she got rid of their table scraps was to yell over the fence and across the orchard for me to come and get 'um. There was many a time I'd duck down so as she couldn't see me when I heard her yellin'. I think Ma made some kind of deal with her that we'd be proud to take them scraps and garbage for the hogs. Most of the time I didn't mind goin' to get the bucket of garbage 'cause she usually gave me a Baby Ruth candy bar 'most anytime I came around. Mr. Lewis was a security guard at the Lorton Penitentiary in Lorton, Virginia and was the only person in the whole wide world that drove slower than Slow Poke Doak. Had somethin' about drivin' over about 10 miles an hour. In the summer time he'd bring home one-gallon cans of blackberries hand picked by the trustees on the road gangs. Ma would swap him one pack of cigarettes per can. That seemed like a pretty good deal to me bein's cigarettes were 20 cents a pack.

The only time I ever hit the Mother Lode back then was when I raked up all the leaves in their yard and hauled 'um off in a gunnysack. Got three 25 cent quarters for doin' that. Mom told me I was takin' advantage of Mrs. Lewis, an elderly and grossly over weight lady, and made me take the money and give it back to her. I told Ma that I had raked the leaves 'cause I didn't have nothin' else to do and that I didn't set no price on the job. Told her the truth - Mrs. Lewis offered me the seventy-five cents. Ma's command: "Give it back". When I went to the house and tried to give the money back, Mrs. Lewis said: "You earned it and I'm not takin' it back". I never worked so hard in my whole life earnin' money that I didn't know I was makin' - try to give it back and then gettin' to keep it. Thought to myself – if this is how Dad earns a livin', it ain't no wonder Mom buys big brother Chip's clothes at the "Not-&-New" consignment shop in Manassas and most all of mine are hand-me-downs!

Manassas was a huge town compared to Clifton. It only had one main street runnin' parallel to the railroad tracks, but the street was pretty long and had a lot of stores on both sides. When it came time to do the weekly shoppin', Ma would drive down across the old one lane Bull Run Bridge which linked Fairfax and Prince William counties. Soon as ya got across the bridge, the county road was a dirt road and went a right smart ways 'til ya hit another paved road. A mile or two before gettin' to Manassas was a little area known as Buckhall. Only thing there was one general store sittin' on the left side of the road where it bent around to the right. On up the road a ways where the road took a 90 degree turn to the left, there were some woods on the right with an old loggin' trail headin' in. Mr. Porter told me there was a place back there he'd take me to someday, where there had been two Indian tribes fightin' it out. Said there was still Indian arrows stuck in the trees there, and he was the only person who knew where it was. That was another one of them things we never got around to doin'.

While Ma did the weekly grocery shoppin' at the Safeway store, us kids were up the street at the Ben Franklin 5 & 10. That store had about anything ya ever wanted. They had a few expensive things as much as a dollar, but 'most everything they had was either 5 or 10 cents. There was a comic book rack that musta' had 25 or 30 to choose from. They had Superman, the Lone Ranger, Hop-A-Long Cassidy and about any other cool comic book you could think of – you name it - they had it! Ben Franklin 5 & 10 was a kids dream come true – not to mention our favorite store for Christmas shoppin' every year. The only other two stores of interest to me were the Western Auto and Southern States, which was serviced by the railroad. Western Auto is where we got bamboo poles for fishin' and my attraction to Southern States was the smell of all the hay and grain stored there.

Half way between Manassas and Centerville was a livestock auction house. Don't remember how often the auctions went on, but that's where Dad bought Abigail, a couple of other cows and the hogs we had on the farm. I never minded too much the smell of a barnyard, so that place was one of my favorites. The structure was mostly hand hewn wooden beams and rafters, with wooden bench seats. There was three things there you could always count on at the auction – a lot of noise, cow-pies and flies. That was one cool place.

The Presbyterian church across the railroad tracks and behind the old boarded up hotel is where I got baptized one night. The preacher was Reverend Howell and he made a big To-Do about the baptisin' of another lost soul. We seldom went to church but did attend Sunday school every Sunday. Mynor McIntyre was not only the Mayor of Clifton but also led us in gospel singin' in the main part of the church every Sunday 'til we broke up into our Sunday school groups. Mr. and Mrs. McIntyre had four kids total. Marvin was the youngest and was my age. He was a little nutty, so naturally, we were best of friends. Malcolm was Kevin and Chip's age and a pretty cool guy. Gwendolyn was the same age as my older sister Karen. Gwen was cute as a bug's ear - long dark hair and all and when she came into full bloom she drove some of us young boys plumb crazy – 'specially me. Charlotte was an adopted daughter that everybody called "Cookie" and was probably my first genuine girlfriend. She was about the same age as me and was as pretty as a picture. With her long brown hair and a good personality - she was about the best of the bunch at Clifton elementary to pick from. I didn't have too much use for the whole church thing back then and couldn't wait 'til it was over. Mom and Dad weren't always there on time to pick us up and while we were killin' time waitin' on 'um, now and again a freight train would come barrelin' down the tracks. A couple of the boys thought it was cool to throw rocks at the windows in the passenger cars. Many a window was busted out of them trains. Chip and I with our good upbringin' and all that religion we'd just got a few minutes prior - would never have considered throwin' a rock at a movin' train even with our excellent throwin' arms and plenty of excess time...or would we.....?

The new Clifton Elementary School was built somewhere around 1953 right smack-dab where the old wooden schoolhouse had stood - up 'til that time. My first grade class was the second or third first grade in the new school and the teacher was Miss Canaster. She was a young good lookin' redhead and was responsible for my first crush on a member of the female species. I used to raise my hand and when she called on me, I told her I had a secret I needed to tell her. When granted permission, I'd go to her desk and she'd pull her long red hair back exposin' her left ear. I never had any such secret to tell her – I just kissed her on the cheek and scurried like a possum back to my desk. She took the bait about three times before catchin' on!!

Every year, 'long about the end of May, Clifton elementary had their annual "May Day" festival. The only cool part of the whole thing was at least we were outdoors practicin' and not in the class room. Kids in the first, second and third grade had to do the May Pole Dance. The way that worked was the teachers put up a pole in the middle of the front yard just outside the first grade class room. There were colorful streamers hangin' from the top of the pole and each kid held one streamer. We stood in a circle all the way around the pole 'bout seven or eight feet from the base. When the music started we were supposed to weave in and out of each other so as to braid the pole. By the time the third graders took their turn, the finished pole wasn't all that bad but it was still one more of them things that worked better in theory than it did on the pole.

The new school was about the biggest building I had ever seen by age six. There were six classrooms, a clinic, the principal's office, a library, a kitchen and an auditorium.

The auditorium also served as the lunchroom. Mom always packed my lunch in a brown paper bag and most days it was the same thing - a peanut butter and jelly sandwich, a banana, and a couple of cookies. She also gave me milk money for when I went through the line in the kitchen. Most days I ate my lunch on the bus on the way to school, so by lunchtime, all I had was a big appetite and the two cents for milk. A good many of the kids (Mostly girls) wouldn't eat all of their lunch so I went from table to table feastin' off the scraps. I hadn't been taught anything about table manners or pride up until then, or if I had - it didn't register, so that system worked pretty good, I always thought.

My second grade teacher, Mrs. Buckley and my third grade teacher Miss Adair were sisters and you'd never known it by lookin' at 'um. Might as well been Mutt and Jeff. Mrs. Buckley was a large, big-boned, heavyset woman and Miss Adair was a little mousey-lookin' thing. Both were ugly as homemade sin and meaner than an alley cat. A kid would have been better off just skippin' those two grades. Sure would have saved a lot of wasted time and two-cents a day milk money. Ain't no tellin' how many times old lady Buckley made me stand in the corner for doin' absolutely nothin' wrong. Miss Adair replaced the standin' in the corner thing with a ruler or a map stick right where she figured it would do the most good. She was the only one figurin' that way, 'cause, none of us kids agreed.

By the fourth grade came Mrs. Block. She was a tall, slim lady with sunken eye sockets covered by a pair of big ol' glasses, long brown hair usually pulled back and spoke with authority. After the last two, Mrs. Block made more sense than a little bit. She was a creative old gal from Front Royal, Virginia and how or why she ended up in Clifton I'll never know. Let me tell you what I mean by creative. 'Long about October she had a plan for each of us to make a Christmas present for our parents. She told us all to bring in two tin cans preferably the size orange juice came in. Next we went out and cut down a cedar tree that was growin' along side the school house just over the line on private property. Cuttin' down the tree was a pretty safe gamble back then on account of people didn't gripe or complain about hardly anything in those days. She brought in a wood saw and we cut the trunk of the tree in slices about an inch and a half thick. Each of us got two slices. She had us clean the slices up real good then shellac both sides 'til they looked presentable. Next we cut the bottom out of the tin cans so they looked 'bout like one of them culverts that water runs through under the road – no top, no bottom. The girls in the class weren't prim and proper or anything like that, but Mrs. Block figured the boys could do a better job of flattenin' out the cans by stompin' on 'um. By the next day all of the flattened tin cans had been painted and were ready for the final touch, which was no more than nailin' them to the bottom of the cedar slices. The contraptions ended up bein' a whole bunch of pairs of home made book ends ready to wrap up and put under the Christmas tree for Mom and Dad. I know one thing – I sure was proud of mine.

Mrs. Block had eyes in the back of her head. I never could figure out how she knew some kid was misbehavin' while she was writin' on the blackboard with her back to the class. She was real good at that. Still don't know the answer to that one but she always knew who the guilty dog was and what he'd done. There's one thing for sure about the old gal, when she took the map stick to your butt it was with authority unlike the love taps of Miss Adair. Kids never told their parents about thrashin's like those back then. Reason was – if the parents found out about the misbehavin', rather than run to the school complainin' about the teacher, they just simply wore his butt out again at home. From a kid's viewpoint that was somethin' like double jeopardy - no trial, no judge and no jury – just down-right payin' up twice for the same crime.

That fourth grade teacher could read like all get out. Now and again she would read a full-length book to the class out loud. Most of the time it took several days 'cause she only read a couple of chapters at a time. Take a book like Tom Sawyer for example. She had a different voice tone for each person – one for Tom, one for Huck, one for Becky and so on. It was all I could do to read the words in a book, let alone change my voice and remember who was who while readin'.

Most young kids like to push a teacher to her limit and if the teacher was dumb enough to let 'um - childish instinct commanded the next level and then the next – kinda' like a squirrel jumpin' from tree to tree. Mrs. Block was with us stride for stride and each time we would try somethin' new, she was always there at the pass headin' us off. We did try gettin' her on one thing though. By fourth grade we were startin' to learn a little bit about the Civil War and we knew that the northerners were called "Yankees" and the southerners were called "Rebels". Bein' from Fairfax County, Virginia we considered ourselves anything but Yankees. Every now and then some kid would ask: "Hey, Mrs. Block are you a Rebel or a Yankee"? That riled her up real good every time. With the pride of a peacock and the defiance of a mockin' bird she'd light into the kid and say: "*I* am an American". Nothin' else, *just that* and then *stare* the kid into the floor. It was probably pledgin' allegiance to the flag every mornin' and things like what I just described that helped make me the halfway decent American citizen that I try to be.

My fifth grade teacher was Norman Fowler. Up until then I always thought teachers had to be females. And one more thing, who would ever name a kid "Norman"? What a goofy name! I just didn't like that guy one bit, period! First of all he was from New Jersey and secondly he was a Philadelphia Philly's fan. Dad always said: "I'm sure there's nice people in New Jersey, but damn if I ever met one". Put that together with the Washington Senators bein' my favorite baseball team and the guy just never stood a chance with me. Even though it was true, Washington was first in war, first in peace but last in the American League - they were my favorite team. The guy was not only ugly but he never said anything worth listenin' to. The fifth grade was a mighty long year for me.

The sixth grade had another male teacher, but this guy was pretty cool. Mr. Arrit, the school principal, was a tall bald-headed guy with a soft voice and commanded respect. He wasn't no pansy either. He talked soft but carried a big stick or however that expression goes. His favorite subject was History and he knew how to teach it.

He was teachin' us about the magnetic poles one time and the next day he brought in about a ten pound magnet to school. It wasn't so much that he brought it to school, but how he did it. He brought the thing in stuck to the side of his car. I gotta' ask you now – how could anyone not like a guy who brought a ten pound magnet to school stuck to the side of his car? Mr. Arrit was a cool guy!

The librarian at Clifton Elementary just happened to be my mother. She kept the place spic and span with every book where it was supposed to be. She called her organization the Huey, Louie or Dewey Decimal System or somethin' like that. When you entered her library it was either don't talk at all or if you must talk – whisper. She had a bunch of magazines on a rack, like "Virginia Wildlife" and "National Geographic". Us boys always grabbed the National Geographic magazine that had the pictures of some Aborigine tribe from somewhere in the world we'd never heard of. We never read any of the text in the magazine, we just looked and giggled at the pictures of all the women with no tops on with their boobies danglin' around. Some of the little girls were startin' to blossom about that time, so maybe it was us boys fantasizin' a little or somethin'. I'm as sure as the stink on a polecat that that was the introduction to the female breast for 'most all of us. One other thing I remember about the library was the year 'long about November when I cut a hornets nest out of a tree and brought it to school. The teacher didn't want the thing in the classroom and told me to take it to the library. 'Long about 10 or 11 o'clock that same day Ma was in a panic. About a dozen hornets came out of hibernation and were flyin' around the room. Since it was all my doin's in the first place – I was instructed to take the thing outside in the cold and dispose of it. That was hard to do bein's I'd gone to a lot of trouble to get the thing out of a tree and it was a pretty cool nest to boot.

Sibling altercations were handled different back in the 50's than they are today. Back then when two boys got mad at each other, the school handled it like Gladiators in the Coliseum. Rather than condone a fist fight, there was two pair of boxin' gloves in the principal's office and when there was no other choice, a fight was scheduled. All the kids would form a ring rather than a square and the boys went at it. That was a dandy way to handle things and usually neither kid won or even got hurt. I don't ever remember brother Chip havin' any boxin' matches though. Reason was, when Chip got pissed he was all over the other boy like a cheap suit, and usually knocked the crap out of the kid before anyone could break it up. The score was settled right then and there in no time flat. Chip was a bad-dude with a short fuse and won every fight he was ever in. That's one reason, I'm glad he was my brother. Although, there was a time when I was about 4 or 5 years old when he shoved me face first into the hardwood floor at the farmhouse and knocked my two front teeth out. Don't recall him bein' mad at me or apologizin' either, so much as just lettin' me know in his tactful way, who was the boss.

After graduatin' from the sixth grade it was time for intermediate school, which was a special school for seventh and eighth graders. We were bussed into Fairfax city to Sidney Lanier School. Sidney Lanier was what ya might call Junior High School and was just around the corner from Kamp Washington where routes 29/211 and route 50 intersected. That was in the western corner area of Fairfax known as Germantown. Leavin' a little ol" country school of about 150 kids and goin' to a big city school with around 1,400 was like expectin' a hound dog to transform into a butterfly. I'd been a big fish in a little pond up 'til then, but this transformation was unbelievable – I'd never seen so many kids in one spot in my whole life. As a matter of fact – I didn't know there was that many kids in the whole world! I felt like such a country bumpkin around all those cool city kids. One of the worst and most embarrassin' moments in my entire life was Home Room period on the first day of school. The teacher had each one of us stand up and recite our name and where we were from. I was around the middle of the pack and with each kid doin' as told, the fatal minute was gettin' closer and closer. Like a fox stalkin' a rabbit, the line just kept gettin' shorter and shorter. I wasn't lackin' no self esteem or anything like that, but how in the heck could I actually tell these cool city kids I was from Clifton? The fox finally went in for the kill – in other words, the spotlight was on me. I stood up and said: "My name is Mike Foley and I'm from (Slur, slur…)" and sat back down. The teacher said: "Where did you say you were from?" I inaudibly slurred it out again. The teacher spoke up again: "I still couldn't understand you. Can you spell that? Now the ax had fallen. I stood up and said "Clifton" in a way that even a deaf idiot could understand. Red faced and embarrassed I sat back down figurin' now all the cool kids would avoid me like the plague.

The country bumpkins from Clifton were accepted as any of the other kids, so maybe I was makin' a bigger deal out of it than I should have. After all, Centerville only had one stop light, a barber shop, Hunter's Hardware store, a gas station, an antique shop, a couple of other little stores and an elementary school. Chantilly wasn't any more than a blinkin' light at a four way crossroads with an old wooden general store on one corner. From the store there was nothin' but either cornfields or hay fields as far as the eye could see – lookin' in any direction. Every now and then you'd see an old wooden farmhouse 'tween there and Centerville – other than that, those areas were just as rural as Clifton – and, possibly even more so. Maybe I was overdoin' it a little - thinkin' I was such a country bumpkin. By the time the dust had settled - us Cliftoners fit in pretty good.

The original Clifton Elementary School
where the current school stands.

The main street of Clifton looking from
Chestnut Street toward the rail road tracks.

Aerial view of Clifton, Virginia - circa 1929.
This is exactly as the town looked in the 1950's
and has changed very little as of today.

Railroad tracks to the left with the
Baptist church lower dead center

A Farm Sure Is Fun

One thing's for sure about livin' on a farm – if'n there ain't nothin' to do – it's your fault. Now that, my friend, is a fact. It's absolutely amazin' how simple and complicated life was livin' on the farm even before the invention of big screen T.V.'s with surround sound or dirt bikes, four wheelers, cell phones and computers. When ya ran out of things to do, ya just thought up somethin' new and went and did it.

One day Chip and Jon and I decided to dig ourselves a swimmin' pool. Ain't rightly sure whose bright idea that was. We picked out a good spot between a couple of pear trees 'long side Jon's driveway and started diggin'. That project took months to do as we weren't gunna' dig no half-assed pool. We dug and dug with pick and shovels 'til we figured we had it about right. By the time we finished, we had ourselves a real genuine swimmin' pool - rectangular in shape - about five feet wide and six feet long and around four and a half feet deep. Bein' on a limited budget and all, the only materials or dependable resources we had were a big idea, shovels, a pick and elbow grease.

When we finally finished up - there she was - a first class, country boy swimmin' pool. The pool didn't have a liner or divin' board – nothin' fancy like that. It didn't have a concrete walkway or a grouted tile rim around it. The pool was just a big ol' hole in the ground with dirt piled all the way around it. It was done – exceptin' for the water. Jon got a garden hose and turned it on full tilt. We ran that hose about an hour or so 'til Jon's mother told us to turn the hose off for fear of runnin' the well dry. Had about a foot of water in the pool at the time. Next day when we came back, all we had was a little mud on the bottom. We didn't know the first thing about water perkin' back then, not even Jon. I reckon we soaked that ground pretty good that day, 'cause not long after that we had a good old fashioned "Gully Washer" of a thunder storm and by-crackie that pool was about two feet deep in water by the time the clouds parted. Thanks to Mother Nature our pool was ready for us boys to try out. None of us had bathin' suits or anything fancy like that, so we just stripped down to our Fruit of the Looms and jumped in. That was our first and last attempt at swimmin' in the pool. Just don't have the heart to ever mention again about them pigs of ours wallerin' in the mud.

'Long about September after hayin' time when the fields were cut and baled and the hay was in the barn, we built us one fine football field on a nice flat spot. First thing we done was go cut six decent trees. Cut all the branches off and trimmed 'um up into long poles. We took the posthole digger and dug two holes. Next thing we had to do was measure 'um up real good then attach the horizontal crossbar pole to the two that would be standin' upright. We fetched us some used balin' wire and pretty soon we had the first of two goal posts layin' right there on the ground. Two of us lifted 'um up while the other made sure the bottoms went right in the holes we'd dug. We straightened the thing up and packed the dirt back in the hole, firmin' it up real good. We paced off a hundred yards and the whole process started again in the end zone closest to our house. By the time we were done, we had a genuine football field just like the Pros – end zones, goal posts and all. One old foldin' yard chair served as both the sideline and the bleachers. Only thing we didn't have was enough players for a team. My sister Karen was three years older than any of us, and bein's she'd started doin' lady-like things – it wasn't much worth even askin' her. Kevin was our only other choice. Tried to coax sister Kevin into formulatin' an interest in bein' a football player, so as to even up the teams. Kevin didn't show much interest, which was just as well, 'cause nobody wanted her on their team anyway – so we were back to the original three.

From time to time, we did get a couple of kids from neighborin' farms to come by and we had some pretty good football games right there in the Jon, Chip and Mike stadium.

The only real memorable football game I recollect was down at Glen Jackson's house in Clifton. We got up a mess of kids for a game that day and chose up teams. The game was tackle football just like ya see on T.V. We didn't need no helmets or pads or any of those unnecessary slow-ya-down things. We came there to play football and we knew what we were doin'. Don't have any idea which team won the game, but there's one thing I do remember. In the middle of one play, me and Dorian Fullerton, crashed heads, full blast. I was pert' near knocked out cold and had to go to the house to have ice bags put on the golf ball sized knot I had right in the middle my forehead. Took about a week for that thing to go down. Nobody on either team ever went on to the NFL, but years later, a couple of us did turn out pretty good at the high school level.

Ol' Jon and Chip and I sure thought up a lot of neat things to do for kids that had to invent their own entertainment. Like the time we decided to build us a cabin down at the lower end of the sleigh run right next to the creek. Picked out a nice spot just inside where the medium sized pine trees started into the woods. We picked there 'cause we didn't want the thing to be too visible from Jon's house or the open fields. Jon's mother was always against everything we done - so just out of sight was the perfect place. Other reason was – buildin' it next to the creek - we'd have plenty of water to drink and not have to be luggin' our canteens. Back in those days when ya got a thirst that needed quenchin', ya just bent over and drank out of whatever creek was near by. Our plan was to build us a cabin for campin' out, meetin' up in or just a place of our own away from the parents. Nothin' elaborate – just one of them places we could call our "Home away from Home" when ya got tired of bein' around all those people that bugged or bored ya.

First thing we put up was the four corner posts. After that came the floor and walls with a door openin'. The roof was last.

Reckon I'm makin' it sound like a pretty simple operation, but it was anything but that. We had to carry the old used lumber, nails and tools a right smart ways. The good part was the luggin' was all down hill goin' to it, but as ya might figure, it was all uphill headin' back home. Chip and Jon were the architects and I was what ya might call the uneducated, cheap help. We cut a bunch of trees and used them here and there. The ol' cabin was kinda' like the swimmin' pool – took just as long to build - and 'bout the time we finished up, we'd done lost interest and moved on to somethin' new.

We did some "Campin' Out" back in those days too. I wasn't along for the maiden voyage - when Chip and Jon camped out in Jon's front yard. Can't remember exactly how the story went, but they got scared or it started rainin' or somethin'. Anyway, they never made it through the night outside and went in the house where they were safe from Mother Nature and/or the Boogie Man.

There was a creek that went right through the middle of our farm. One of the fields had a high bluff that tapered down to a little flat spot at the creek. Dad named that hill, "Pat's Hill" on account of Mom and we named the little flat spot, "Fairy Land". When we were big and brave, say by age 10 or 11, we camped out at that spot two or three times. There was a really steep embankment on the other side of the creek that dropped off nearly straight down. We'd go up through the woods to the top and slide down that thing right to the creek. Slidin' down that hill was about as much fun as anything I remember. We had a couple of those ol' drab, grasshopper green army surplus pup tents that we pitched and then built a little campfire. Ice coolers hadn't come along yet and Coleman lanterns were way too expensive, so any food had to be eaten that night or it was gunna' go bad. We'd all gotten past the "Chicken" stage about campin' out and there was such a thing as safety in numbers anyway, so if anyone was scared he wasn't about to let on. There's just somethin' that can't be described in words about how cool it is to be listenin' to the whippoorwills and katydids while cookin' marshmallows over a campfire.

Another time we went campin' up the road about two miles. We cut down a side dirt road a ways to where somebody had a chain locked up across a driveway leadin' off it. It was pretty obvious that nobody lived back there full time with the leaves and sticks all over the narrow cow path driveway. We moseyed on back to where a small house was built on a point of land where Occoquan River was headin' on downstream right past a quiet little cove. We pitched our tents and built us a campfire right in the guys yard closest to the river. Chip decided he was gunna' do him some night fishin'. The boy still brags about that bluegill he caught on jitterbug fishin' lure. That sure was a great campsite but the only problem was, luggin' all our stuff two miles each way. I went back to that spot several different times and never did see hide nor hair of the owner. Doubt the guy woulda' minded us campin' there even if we had asked permission – people back then just somehow got along and never complained about too much.

At the farm there was a loggin' road that went back in the woods a couple of hundred yards or so to an old saw mill. It hadn't been shut down long when we moved to the farm judgin' by the size of the sawdust pile and the scrap wood all piled up in a heap. The old belt driven saw was still there but the ol' hit and miss flywheel that made it spin was gone. That woodpile is where Dad took us when we were real little to teach us how to shoot the 22 rifle. We put tin cans up in the woodpile and shot at them from 40 feet or so.

Years later Chip and I set up another shootin' range just past the pig pen. There was two hills with a ravine like dip between 'um. We'd stand over on the hill where the woods were and shoot at targets across the way. One Sunday when

Mom and Dad weren't around, the Bowman's came a callin'. They brought some heavy artillery with 'um and we were fixin' to do some serious shootin' that day. Robby Bowman and I had started collectin' Civil War bullets and artifacts a few years earlier. Bullets were plentiful down around the flat parts of Bull Run when the water level was down. 'Cause they'd been under water and all, the patinas were white as a snow flake and easy to spot. We had a bunch of different guns that day and one was a black powder, muzzle loadin' reproduction of a 50-caliber Civil War Colt pistol. There was a stump at the wood line. I decided to fire a Minnie ball into it at point blank range and then fire another one in the same spot. In theory, if done just right, the second would crash into the first one and they'd be stuck together appearin' the two had collided in mid air when a Reb' and a Yank' were shootin' at each other. Everybody seemed to agree it looked pretty good on the drawin' board. I fired the first one perfectly then put a double charge of powder in the pistol for the second shot so as to increase the wallop and hopefully make the two stick together. Only problem was – I missed the first one and hit a knot in the stump. The second shot ricocheted back and hit me right above the left eye. I was down for the count and the bullet hit me so hard a knot jumped out on my forehead so big that everyone thought the bullet was under the skin. A few ice packs later, I was back to my semi- normal self again.

The next day I was doin' the ol' firecracker trick. I was puttin' Black Cat firecrackers in beer bottles along the road and throwin' 'um up in the air to watch 'um explode. "Bout the time I had it down real good, one exploded in my hand before I could heave it. Now, *that* was about a mess. The busted glass cut my throwin' hand and also cut me up side the head in a few places. When the Bowman boys were around we just had to do everything the cool way - on the edge or nothin'.

One other little story about shootin' guns. What I'm gettin' ready to tell ya right now, I've never told anybody about in all my pea pickin' days. Out the back door of the farmhouse about 30 paces or so was a bird feeder. It was a flat piece of wood on a post with an "A" framed roof. The 'ol farm cats used to hang out around the back door 'cause that's where we fed 'um and it bein' on the west side of the house, wasn't all that bad a place to be on a winter afternoon. I was in charge of the bird feedin'. Wasn't much to it most of the time but after a big snow storm I had to dig out a path to it, clean it off then clear a decent sized spot on the ground around it for the birds. After it snowed it always seemed there was 10 times as many birds at the feeder than usual. That was good. What was bad was you could always count on a bunch of nasty 'ol Bluejays hoggin' the feeder and not lettin' the other little birdies have anything to eat. I solved that problem. When no one was home but me, I used to go upstairs to my sisters' bed room which was on the same side of the house as the feeder. I'd open the window up a little bit and with the 22 rifle I'd pick 'um off the feeder one at a time. The cats picked up on that trick real quick and with a path already through the snow to the feeder, I didn't even have to go get 'um.

I knew every square inch of our farm and just about the same for everybody else's, within reason. I never owned a compass and never had a need to either. A country boy learns early how to determine where he is, at any given time by where the sun is in the sky or which way the wind's blowin', so as not to get lost in the woods. The wind might change directions – but, the moss always grows on the north side of the tree and the sun always sets in the west. I don't ever remember gettin' lost. From time to time when I'd be in a new area, I could always count on there bein' a hound dog howlin' or a tractor plowin' a field or something like that 'bout the time I was headin' out. It was always prudent to be mindful of your surroundin's. Even if someone blindfolded ya up, then spun ya around a few times then took ya down through the hollow and up the next ridge, before taking the blindfold off – one thing was as certain as a tick on a hound dog - that mutt was still carryin' on and the tractor was still plowin' and neither one had moved much from where they were at. On a chilly day in the fall, you could count on the blackbirds always headin' south or flocks of geese headin' in from the northwest. A rooster crowin' or a cow mooin' weren't bad benchmarks either when it came to not gettin' lost.

A country boy just always seemed to do what he had to do – even though, sometimes it wasn't necessary to do, but he did it anyway. That fact bein' stated - it was always good to know what you were doin' when you were doin' somethin' – that most likely didn't need doin' in the first place - and where you were at when you were doin' it was important too. Where you were at and what you was doin' - played a big part in the doin' - if ya see what I'm gettin' at. I 'most always knew what I was doin' and where I was at – and that's a fact – for the most part.

There was one exception to all that worldly knowledge when it came to doin' what didn't need doin'. 'Long about age 5 or 6, I was walkin' down the road one day and came onto a culvert 'bout the size of a basketball - runnin' under the road. Curiosity took holt to me and I just had to find out if I could see all the way through it from one side of the road to the other - about 12 to 14 feet total. Seemed there was somethin' blockin' the view and it was movin' around just a little bit. I was determined to get that thing out of the way, so I threw a rock at it, best I could, to chase it on out the other end. 'Bout that time a skunk cut loose on me 'til he was plumb satisfied. When I got home I stunk so bad that Ma made me strip down in the yard before she put me in the tub. She didn't get after me too much due to the fact that accidents been known to happen.

After gettin' cleaned up with clean clothes and all, I went back outside wanderin' around and thinkin' about this and that. Couldn't help but wonder if the polecat was still in the culvert and I had to find out. Figured I'd be careful takin' a gander this time around. Well guess what – that son-of-gun was still there and waitin' on me. He drew a bead this time like he was shootin' a rifle and hit the bulls-eye better the second time then he did the first. When I got home stinkin' for the second time, I damn sure wasn't Ma's favorite of us four kids that day!

I could go on and on 'til the cows come home about country boy things and doins' back in the 50's. Things like buildin' lean-to's, tree forts, fishin' at the Run, catchin' lightin' bugs and the like, but I think you got the general idea of what life was like back then. That was a good life, a fun life and a clean life (Not countin' our clothes or polecats). Unfortunately though, it's a life I ain't seen the likes of in many a year - and may no longer even exist.

Duffy was a Gentleman

I hope you're payin' attention real good, 'cause I got something to tell you 'bout right now! Ol' Duffy was smarter than most any person I'd ever come across in all my pea pickin' days. Duffy wasn't much of a talker but he sure could sing. Favored Country & Western, I guess ya could say, but the only problem was – he always sang the same song. Ya probably remember that old country song called "Cattle Call", well, that was his song and, boy oh boy, could he sing it! Whenever we put the record on, Duffy would sing along 'til it was over. Now and again we'd get tired of the tune - but most of the time we encouraged him to sing.

In all my years roamin' around from here to there, I've run across some pretty tough Dudes, but Duffy was the badest of the bads. He didn't go around lookin' for a fight, but one thing's for sure, if one came his way, chances were the other guy was fixin' to get whooped. He was so rough and tough he could whoop 'most any man or beast. 'Though only medium in stature, he wouldn't hesitate to challenge anything twice his size. If there'd ever been anything like a "Club for the Bad Boys", I guarantee Duffy would have been the boss. When anyone or anything ever messed with me – Duffy would always jump right in - takin' up for me - even though he was three and a half months my junior.

Duffy was a kind and gentle soul. He was loyal and protective of those he loved and he never asked or begged for nothin'. He was a handsome rascal with a twinkle in his eye, teeth white as an Easter Lilly and a handshake of patience and sincerity. When ya shook hands with that guy it was more than just shakin' hands to be shakin' hands – it meant somethin'. Trust and honor were a big deal to him. He was just as popular with the girls as he was with the guys. When he was right, he was right. And he was 'most always right by virtue of natural intelligence and common sense, but when he was wrong – he'd take a scoldin' with the honor and pride of a true gentleman.

Another thing about Duffy – he was fast on his feet. In a regular ol' foot race neither Chip nor I stood a chance. One time on our way to the dump Dad was drivin' the tractor through the lespedeza field rather than the dirt road. Dad decided on lespedeza that year rather than corn. He said somethin' about rotatin' the crops was good for the soil or somethin' like that. Dad just did things sometimes for no particular reason the way I saw it. We'd gone over the flat part on the topside of the field and were headin' down a gradual slope. Chip and I were hangin' on like usual. Duffy wasn't much for ridin' on the tractor so he just always ran along instead. Felt more comfortable on foot I guess and it was good exercise in the fresh country air. Anyway, at the base of the slope about 40 paces ahead of us was a wild turkey hen runnin' through the knee high lespedeza draggin' one wing. Appeared to me she'd broke a wing somehow and couldn't fly. She was almost to the dirt road when the tractor got to where she had started out. 'Bout that time around 7 or 8 baby turkeys took off like a mismanaged covey of quail. The little turkeys were about the size of a banty rooster and couldn't fly no more than about ten yards at a clip. When they hit the ground, they'd take off runnin' for a spell and then glide again. Didn't take no coaxin' for us boys to come flyin' off the tractor in a foot race to catch one of those little guys. Problem was, every time we almost had one, they'd take off and glide. When we caught up again, they'd glide again. By the time they made it to the woods – they were home free! Ain't rightly sure whatever happened to Duffy in all that confusion. Anyway, we went on to the dump, took care of bustin' bottles and gettin' rid of the trash then headed on home. Found out later that the ol' broken wing thing was a trick of nature that wild turkeys do to try to get you to chase them 'stead of their young. Mother Nature sure can be creative sometimes. Somewhere 'round a half hour after we got home, here comes Duffy. Ol' Duffy had his baby turkey in his mouth.

Duffy was born on May 28, 1948. He was an Irish Terrier and the best damn dog there ever was – and that's a fact! Mom and Dad swore that I learned to walk holdin' on Duffy's tail. I can't vouch for that one but they claim it's true. Knowin' Duffy, it probably was true. I always thought Duffy was smarter then me and I know damn well he was smarter than Chip.

Did ya ever know one of those guys that people just like to mess with and aggravate? Well, Duffy was one of those guys.

Every now and then on one of those beautiful Spring or Fall afternoons, Duffy would just lay out in the middle of the yard soakin' up the sunshine and take himself a good old fashion snooze. We had two white ducks, Emmy and Lou, that wandered around the barnyard or wherever they felt like wanderin'. We never caged 'um up, I suppose 'cause they never went anywhere more than a couple hundred feet or so in any direction. They had this thing for Duffy when he was mindin' his own business and just takin' it easy nappin' in the yard. Those ducks were triflin' little devils. 'Bout the time they were sure he'd dozed off, they'd sneak up on him and peck him real good and take off runnin'.

Most of the time Duffy just put up with their baloney. One particular day, Duffy had enough of their shenanigans and took off after 'um. He grabbed one of 'um by the neck and snapped it 'til the damn thing's soul was on it's way to ducky heaven. Dad never knew the particulars of the incident and figured Duffy had done wrong. He took the dead duck and beat the poor dog with it unmercifully. Duffy didn't run – he just stood there and took the beatin' like a man. After the beatin', Dad took a piece of rope and tied the dead duck around Duffy's neck. Like I said before, Duffy knew right from wrong, so in a humiliatin' kinda' way, he just moped around for the rest of the day with the real culprit danglin' in the breeze. Ol' Duff never even tried to get that Albatross from around his neck – he just paid his dues for defendin' himself and figured that tomorrow would be a better day. Don't ever recall knowin' a man with that much tolerance or class.

Bein's Duffy was so smart, we figured all Irish Terriers were smart. Pushin' our luck one day, Mom and Dad decided to get Duffy a girl friend. Maggie was a bitch terrier and 'though I don't recall the particulars, somehow ended up belongin' to my older sister Karen. Most likely it was another one of them birthday things like the two hogs. Well, I'm gunna lay another fact of life on ya right now. All terriers ain't smart! Maggie was dumb as a fence post. She just wandered around like the "Lost Souls of Purgatory", peed on the floor and never paid ya much mind when spoken to. Duffy was an easy goin' kinda' guy and just put up with her like some guys do their wife. "Bout the only credit I could ever give ol' Maggie – she was good breedin' stock. She gave up several litters of good pups before her untimely death. Maggie had a good Irish heart, but man, was she stupid.

Back to Duffy. I could tell ya Duffy stories for a month of Sundays. Like the time he got into it with a skunk for example. Nobody saw the scrap actually happen but we were sure there was one dead polecat out there someplace. It's a good thing that happened at the right time of year when the weather was nice - 'cause Duffy wasn't allowed back in his own house for a week or better.

Another time a stray dog came into the yard. Have no idea where that dog came from, especially since I thought I knew personally every dog within a five-mile radius. He and Duffy were almost the exact same size. When Duff spied the stranger trespassin' - there was no time for small talk – he was on that Son-of-a-gun like a rooster on a June Bug - and the fight was on. The black stranger held his own for a while - but only a while. Duffy literally tore that creature to shreds. I've seen a few dogfights in my time but never one so vicious. Rather than kill the intruder

55

right there, 'tween the bush and the screened in porch, big-hearted Duffy allowed him to live another day as the mutt hobbled out of the yard, across the road and into the woods. Never saw a dog so torn up and still walkin' in all my life.

Another memorable scrap was one frosty November mornin'. Slow Poke Doak was about due and when we came out the front door fixin' to get on the bus in a minute or so - there was a big ol' raccoon right in the middle of the blue stone driveway about ten feet this side of the tool shed. Duffy spotted him and took off after him. I've always believed a good redbone or even a coonhound was no match for a big coon, one on one, and Duffy was nowhere near the size of either. Matter of fact, Duffy was closer to the size of the coon than either of dogs just mentioned. Anyway, the coon took up under the corncrib and Duff was right on his heels. That fight was the most ferocious and nastiest soundin' thing I think I ever heard right up to this day. There's an old poem called: "The Gingham Dog and the Calico Cat" I once read, where the fight was so bad that the two actually ate each other up. Always seemed to me that one would eat the other and I never could figure how both ate each other up. Anyway, that's how the poem went. Long and the short of the whole thing – that's what I figured might happen this time too. That fight seemed it would never end and there was growlin', hissin', screamin', bangin' and the worst kind of thrashin' around a body ever heard. The corncrib floor tapered back with the wide part where Chip and I were tryin' to see what was goin' on. We didn't have a very good view but we sure could hear what was happenin'. That was the only time in my life I was ever feared for ol' Duff.

I'd of helped Duffy if I could 'cause I knew this was gunna' be a fight to the finish and there was only goin' to be one winner this time around – somebody was gunna' die. After about a half hour things started slowin' down a tad and us two boys still didn't have any idea who was winnin'. In time we heard somethin' crawlin' out, kinda' comin' our way. Fancy that! Damn if it wasn't ol' Duffy! When the boy came out he was torn to ribbons. He had cuts and chomp holes all over him. If anyone ever questioned Duffy's manhood or pride, listen here to what happened next. When he got all the way out he just stood there right between Chip and me with his Irish head in the air like nothin' had ever happened. He was hurtin' real bad - had to been just lookin' at him - but he didn't want us to know. After about a minute or so, Duff walked over to the big oak tree off the back corner of the crib, cocked his leg and peed right on the tree. Then he went back up under the corncrib to where the fight had taken place, grabbed the dead raccoon and dragged him out. Duffy strategically laid him down right there at our feet. I was always proud of anything Duffy ever done, but I was a little prouder of him that day.

Dad always said that Duffy could understand the English language, so most of the time I'd make careful sure not to say the wrong thing in his presence. For example, I'd brag about my dog at school but I was real careful never to call Duffy a dog to his face. And if ya think he didn't know arithmetic – try stickin' three Milk Bones in your pocket and then only give him two. Duffy wasn't a dog – he was a member of the family. To call him a dog sorta' put him in the same class as them four redbone hound puppies Dad brought home one time. When they grew up we kept 'um in a big homemade wire pen out back of the corncrib. Those mutts were good ol' huntin' dogs alright, but no class. All they ever did was howl and eat about a hundred pounds of dog food a week between 'um. We ended gettin' rid of 'um one by one and in a little while I'll tell you 'bout the best of the bunch – Smokey.

Duffy, as good as he was didn't live the perfect life though. One time he got hit by a motorcycle and got his back leg broke. A few years later an old goofy mule we had at the farm named Jake the Flake, kicked him in the same leg and broke it again. As he started gettin' up in the years that leg took ta' gettin' weak and his back end started cavein' in. Next thing to give out was his eye sight due to cataracts and then his hearin' went almost deaf. His teeth started fallin' out not long after all that. Later in his life I had to carry him up and down the stairs in the house because no matter where we were he always wanted to be with us. It was hard on me watchin' that wonderful member of our family fall apart right before my eyes. Mom always knew when the time was right for this, that or the other. One day when no one was around Ma took Duffy to the vet and had him put to sleep. Ma took care of that painful deed all by herself so as to save the rest of the family the heartache and sorrow of that pitiful undertakin'. Mom was a strong woman and she always seemed to know the right time for everything – good or bad. Bet ya two more coke bottles she was right too, 'cause I know I couldn't have even rode along in the car, let alone do it all by myself. I cried like a baby when I found out - even though I knew it was the right thing to do. The thought of never seein' Duffy again was more than I could handle, especially since he was not only my first dog but my first love too. Duffy left our family at age sixteen.

And one more thing – Duffy was a Gentleman.

Karen and Duffy somewhere around 1950 in Bay Ridge, Maryland

The duck devils, Emmy and Lou

Duffy stretching it out

Workin' on the Farm

If ya live on a farm there's a lot of work to do. When we first moved to the farm, us kids were too little to do much more than straighten up our bedrooms. The bigger we got, the more work we were given to do.

Dad was workin' in Rosslyn, Virginia just this side of the Key Bridge from Georgetown, D.C. Back then there was no beltway and no shortcuts from Clifton to Rosslyn. Mostly back roads 'til he got to Falls Church and then congestion the rest of the way. Dad stayed over many a night because the drive was just too much. On the weekends he had to rest up for the next week, so other than ride around on his tractor, he didn't do none too much fieldhand workin' type of work. Can't say as I blamed him, but the work did need to get done - accordin' to him anyway.

There was a teenaged boy up the road named David Berry. David came from a poor, but proud, family and 'less he got himself a job he had no money. David was a handsome, well-mannered and strong young man. The boy was no stranger to the nastiest kinda' workin' jobs either. He was an ambitious youngster with above average intelligence and he knew if'n he ever went to college he'd have to earn the money himself. Mom and Dad made a deal with him to work on the farm after school and on weekends. The work was nasty but the pay was good – 50 cents an hour. David did anything he was asked to do and did a damn good job of it. He wasn't into complainin' about or refusin' some crappy job either.

David did it all – cut brush, fix fences and even painted the barn roof with creosote. One day after school he was creosotin' the barn roof and fell off. The bucket of that nasty stuff came right down with him and covered him from head to toe. That was 'bout the first time in my life I ever saw a black man. Ma helped clean him up as best she could and got him home. David was the workin'est guy I think I ever saw. He walked to our house and then back home since he didn't have transportation. He saved up enough money one summer to buy himself a car. It was some old junk car from back in the 30's but it did run, and he called it a jalopy. Jalopy or no jalopy, he was ridin' and that beat walkin' two miles 'round trip any day.

One day Ma sent David on some job way back on the back side of the farm. Chip and I went with him. Dad had an old 1950 Ford short bed, flair side pickup truck with a six cylinder engine and three speeds on the column. That was about the only way they came back then. We were on that same dirt road leadin' to the dump and almost to the crest of that hill where we saw the turkey hen doin' the broken wing trick. The truck was stopped in the middle of the road and David was loadin' it up with brush or fence boards or something like that. Anyway, he needed the truck moved up a smidgen and asked if Chip and I thought we could do it. We were mighty little at the time so he told Chip to stand on the seat and hold the steerin' wheel and yank the gear shifter down. He told me to get down on the floor and push the big pedal real easy-like. I didn't know any more about easy-like than Chinese arithmetic. Chip did his part just fine but I hit the gas pedal way too hard. I had no idea what was goin' on, 'cause I was down there on the floor supposedly doin' as told. The truck went over that hill and was headin' for the woods full blast. Fortunately, David ran track in high school and was pretty fast on his feet. He took off after the runaway truck, jumped on, opened the door and stopped it just before we crashed into the woods. Only other thing I remember 'bout that occurrence was, David, out of breath, sayin': "Thanks boys, next time I'll do it myself".

To the best of my recollection, I do believe my older sister Karen was sweet on David. He was a couple of years older than her and had that "Older Man" attraction or somethin'. In the summer David worked with no shirt on and with his dark hair, toned muscles and a sun tan, I guess he was attractive to a young farm girl. Any time he was workin' anywhere near the house, Karen was always there – talkin' to him and, I guess, distractin' him. She was mighty quick to get him a glass of cold water or Koolaid any time he asked. David was never rude, mean or impolite to the young lass who was always lookin' at him with "Googie Eyes" and was never short of a whole lot of small talk.

As the years went by, David had saved enough money to go to college and did just that. One day, Mom sent Chip and me down to the barn to clean out the horse stall. The horse biscuits were about a foot deep and the job was about a nasty one. I remember Chip sayin' right in the middle of the job: "I just don't understand why that lazy "Son-of-a-...." had to go off to college. I think I came back with somethin' like: "'Probably 'cause he figured Ma was fixin' to give him this job".

David Berry had his head screwed on straight and knew what he wanted in life. He was an honest and hard workin' young man. He not only did go off to college, but graduated from college and as of this day and story, owns and runs his own Pharmacy in Kingsport. Tennessee.

In the yard we had two Hickory trees, a huge Gum tree, a Catawba and three Mimosas. In the fall there wasn't none too few leaves to rake. Bein' that rakin' time was shortly before Christmas, Mom and Dad paid us to rake the leaves. They got the rakin' part done free - the deal was 2 cents per gunny sack full for takin' 'um to the compost pile 'round back of the corn crib. Kevin had a couple of good hidin' places where you could always fine her leanin' on the leaf rake. Claimed she was takin' a break. She didn't mind haulin' the leaves for the 2 cents part of the deal, but, her gunny sack was never more than half full. Bein's she was a girl, us boys never made a big To-Do about it. Sometimes we raked the leaves in the driveway into a big pile and burned them. There's somethin' about the smell of burnin' leaves that you never forget once ya done smelt' it. I never minded the smell of a barnyard or a pigpen - and they are distinct in themselves, but burnin' leaves – that's a smell sweeter than home made apple pie.

I reckon Kevin had a thing against rakin' leaves due to all the Hickory nuts and Gum balls layin' there amongst 'um. The leaves were nothin' to rake up, but the Hickory nuts and the Gum balls were a pain in the neck. Dad always told us: "A job worth doin' is worth doin' right", to which Chip or I usually chirped back: "Yeah Dad, but this job ain't worth doin'". Made no difference, if he was shellin' out 2 cents a gunny sack, the job better be done right. 'Long about mid-November, we had that yard lookin' good in their estimation – we never minded the leaves bein' there, but the two cents a bag wasn't all that bad.

As for the leaf pile back behind the corncrib - by crackie, that was one heap of leaves. We dumped the leaves right on top of last year's leaves, which were compostin' away by that point. Down in the old rotted up compost pile, were the biggest night crawlers and the best fishin' worms in the whole wide world. When we put that natural compost in the gardens in the spring, we'd get humongous tomatoes and squash every year. Ma always said that natural compost was better fertilizer than anything store bought. Well, like the ol' saying goes: "The proof of the puddin' is in the tomatoes", or somethin' like that - and how true that was. We had more fun playin' "King of the Mountain" on that compost pile when cluttered with fresh leaves than you could ever imagine. We even climbed the Walnut tree just behind the tool shed to get up on the roof and then jump off into the leaves. Remember now, country boys had to create their own entertainment and that was entertainment. If ya think that sounds corny – don't criticize it 'til ya try it!

We never did get to the point where all the work was done out at the farm. 'Bout the time we thought we were finished up, either Mom or Dad done found somethin' new that needed doin'. Like in the summertime when we had to clip the hedge or mow the lawn for example. Mowin' such a big yard wasn't easy with a push mower. We'd take turns with the mowin'. When Chip got tired of pushin' the lawn mower, he'd say: "Hey Mike, spell me". Well, that's exactly what I did, I said: "It's spelled, M-E". He didn't think that was very funny and usually just walked away with the mower runnin' for me to take over.

Chip did most of the hedge clippin' and all we had back then was a pair of those old fashioned manual clippers. By the time the hedge needed clippin', it was most of the time pretty shaggy to where ya couldn't see through it. 'Most every year the yellow jackets or hornets would lay claim to a good spot and build a nest. The bad part of that deal was you never knew where the nest was 'til they started gettin' after ya. One year the yellow jackets built a big ol' nest at the end of the hedge closest to the top of the driveway. Now, that's where them bees made a big mistake. Dad used to say: "The idle mind is the devils workshop". I reckon Chip and I had some pretty idle minds back then, cause we were always thinkin' up somethin'. What we did was throw rocks at the nest from the car, which was about 10 feet away, and then roll the windows up real fast. Betcha that car got stung a thousand times. Chip didn't have a drivers license or anything yet, but he did know how to back the car up good enough to get out of range of the pissed off bees. We'd get out of the car and laugh like the idiots we were. Never did get stung.

Another year there was a huge hornets nest in one of the apple trees in the orchard. By mid summer the Walnut tree

I was tellin' ya about a few minutes ago had some halfway decent sized walnuts on it. We'd shake a few off the tree and throw 'um at the hornets nest. The nest was within throwin' distance but out of stingin' distance and we both had damn good throwin' arms. The best part of the whole deal was the nest was far enough away that the bees didn't know who was messin' with 'um. I don't believe hornets have ears either, or if they do their hearin' ain't so good. Reason I say that is - one of us would make a killer shot with a walnut and usually say something like: "Got that-Son-of-a-....., dead-center" then laugh like Hell!

Never was a year we didn't have a hornet's nest or two around somewhere. Most of the time it was up under the eve of the barn roof on the outside. 'Long about July when the nest was about the size of a basketball, it was time to take action. We'd get ourselves a long pole and tie a bunch of rags on one end real good. We'd wait 'til after dark and put on a wide brim hat with cheese cloth draped over it and tucked into a heavy coat. Used cheese cloth 'cause we could see out it and the hornets couldn't get to us.

Next we doused the rags in kerosene and lit it with a match. Then we took the long pole and held the burnin' part to the front door hole of the nest. Reason for the front door hole is to prevent them from gettin' away 'cause hornet nests don't have no back door. A hornets nest takes a good while to burn, 'bout twenty minutes or better. When we figured we had the job done, we'd leave and put the burnin' rags out. That technique 'most always worked.

One particular year when we thought we'd done got 'um all, we went on in the house and went to bed. A couple of weeks later we noticed the nest was comin' back and got bigger and bigger every day. The really peculiar thing this time was, it had two holes, one on each side. I ain't never seen a hornets nest with two holes and I don't expect a prudent person to believe the story, but, there's still a few of us around who saw it and will testify to the fact that I ain't lyin'. Dad always said: "Necessity is the mother of invention" and I guess that applies to hornets too.

Speakin' of hornets nests, about the coolest one I ever saw in my whole life was up the road at the Detwilers house. Old man Landis was a plumber by trade and had the cussin'est mouth God ever put on a human bein'. He couldn't communicate without cuss words in every sentence. Mom and Dad didn't think too much of us kids bein' around him, figurin' he was a bad influence on us, or somethin'. When the well pump would go out or some other plumbin' problem, there was no one else to call. After he was done with the job, he'd always hang around talkin' about this, that or the other. That's the part Mom and Dad didn't think so much of. Couldn't be rude though, after all, your neighbors were your neighbors, and every now and again ya needed 'um for somethin'.

That one year the hornets went and built a nest right in the middle of a pane glass window on one of the Detwiler's sheds. The nest was huge - probably somewhere around a foot and a half long. The coolest part of the deal was where you could go inside the shed and watch the bee thing from the inside. Always wondered what they were doin' inside the nest – now I know.

Sunday afternoons were whitewash time. Mom and Dad always dropped us kids off Sunday mornin's at the Presbyterian church in Clifton. They made us go to Sunday School every Sunday when we were kids. They usually went to visit their dear friends the Tolson's for an hour or so, then come back and pick us up. Our Sunday tradition was to stop at Price's store on the way home and get 25 fireballs. We each got four. I never was too good with arithmetic and all, but, 6 times 4 equals 24 not 25 – I think Dad kept the extra one for himself – after all, he was entitled to it bein's he was the one payin' for 'um. Time we got home and had changed out of our Sunday-go-to-meeting clothes, Dad put us to work white washin' the trees in the yard. That's one job I couldn't stand. White wash is a lime-based solution and a whole lot thinner than regular ol' paint. We'd white wash the base of every tree in the yard from the ground up about three and a half feet. It did make the trees look pretty cool, but every time it rained it was time to do it all over again. We also had a rock-lined driveway and we had to white wash the rocks too. 'Bout the time the lawn was mowed and the trees were white washed, that place really did look pretty sharp.

We used to grow 15 or 20 acres of corn every year. In the fall when it was corn cuttin' time we used to do it by hand with a corn knife then pile 'um in shucks. A corn shuck was where ya cut 60 or 70 corn stalks and stood 'um up leanin' against each other in a tee-pee lookin' formation. After the whole field was done we had to go back and tear the shucks apart and pull the corn off one ear at a time then throw 'um in a pile. Next thing was to come by with the tractor and trailer and pick up the corn ear piles. We'd store the ears in the corn crib 'til we could take them to the

Southern States place over in Manassas and have the corn ground up, corn cob and all into grain for feedin' the cows and horses in the winter.

We raised pumpkins in the same cornfields. One of the most memorable sights of childhood was lookin' at a field of corn shucks and pumpkins on a frosty fall mornin'. You never see those kinda' things anymore - but they've stuck in my mind's eye all these years as vividly as if I was just lookin' at 'um yesterday.

Dad wanted me and Chip to build him a fence one time. Said if we'd build a three board fence the length of the road, stretchin' down from the house to the end of the field, he's pay us $25.00 each when the job was done. That sounded like a deal to me, 'specially when the most we'd ever made for doin' anything was the 2 cents each for them gunny sacks of leaves. We set out a workin' the next day. First thing was to dig the post holes about eight feet apart. Couldn't do but a few at a time or you'd get out of whack when it came to linin' 'um up right. Next thing was to creosote the bottom of the fence post where they went into the ground, so as they wouldn't rot. When we put the post in the ground we had to eye-ball 'um in to make sure they were straight. Then we pounded the boards on with hammer and nails. Don't ever recall doin' more than 3 or 4 sections in any given day. After the boards were on, we had to paint them white and that was the lousiest part of the whole job. Seemed like you'd paint all day and never get anywhere. If I'd known it was goin' to take us all summer to do that job, I'd of asked ol' Dad for an extra 5 bucks. When we were 'bout done with the job, we were paintin' down at the lower end one day when I got the bright idea to paint my initials real big right in the middle of the road. The county had paved the road by then so I painted me a big "M.F." from one side of the road all the way to the other. I was right proud of that art-work and it stayed there for years. As a matter of fact, those initials were still there the day we moved off the farm.

I could probably go on and on about cuttin' weeds along the fence rows, fixin' fences, cleanin' stuff up and the like, but itemizin' them things might get pretty borin'. The long and short of the whole thing is - work never ends on a farm and by the time us kids were in our mid-teens we were happier than Hell to move to the city.

But Dad, Jon Said….

The farm across the way belonged to the Fadelys. They were good 'ol hard workin' folks and about as decent a neighbor as anyone could have asked for. Fred Fadely was a mailman servicin' the Fairfax Station, Virginia area and as I recall a humble man of few words. Mrs. Fadely was an elementary school teacher at Fairview Elementary School also located at Fairfax Station. Fairfax Station wasn't a town but an area and the only thing there was a Catholic church and a railroad junction with a few houses scattered around. The place was up the road a piece, maybe five or six miles from the farm. The church and the slopin' hillside above the rail stop served as a field hospital durin' the Civil War and the area was loaded with Civil War artifacts. Ever hear the old expression: "Bite the Bullet"? Not sure that's where that came from but there were a good many bullets found there with teeth marks in the lead. "Most any bullet found there made it's way to Fairfax Station in some guy's arm or leg. When they amputated the limb they had the guy bite down on a bullet so as not to scream and that's why some of the bullets had teeth marks. One other tid-bit of history there – remember ol' Clara Barton? She's the girl that started the Red Cross thing, case ya didn't know. Well, it just so happens the Fairfax Station field hospital is where Clara Barton started her medical career. That rail line headin' south stretched all the way back down to Richmond, Virginia, the Confederate Capitol, and went through Clifton and on to Manassas lookin' north. Mrs. Fadely was obviously educated beyond high school and well spoken. Jon was their only son 'till he was about twelve or thirteen years old and then out of nowhere came his little brother Charles. Not all that certain Charles was the result of family plannin' - it's just one of them things that happens now and again like a snow-storm in October.

The Fadely farm and our farm had a common boundary line for a right good ways. There was an old rusted barbed wire fence that separated the two fields kinda' like the center line divides the right side of the road from the left, but then, that left and right thing, all depends on which way you're headin' if you know what I mean. So to say that the Fadelys lived on the right side of the fence and we lived on the left was about the same as them sayin' they lived on the left side and we lived on the right. Anyway, the fence separated the two farms if you see what I'm gettin' at. That old fence started at the top of the hill, just beyond the pig pen, where we used to target shoot the rifles into the other hill and stretched across the field past where the hay stack stood for feedin' the cows, then down the hill, with our woods on one side and the remainder of their field on the other. It stretched on down to the creek, where we used to catch frogs and into the woods for a right good ways. Just why that fence went into the woods I never understood. They say good fences make good neighbors and I'll go along with all that - 'til the fence went off into the woods and then the good neighbor thing just didn't make no sense – least ways to me.

Right in the middle of the fence where it crossed the two fields was our rendezvous point. "Lassie" was a popular T.V. show in the 50's and, as you may or may not recall, Timmy had a friend across the way. When they needed to get together, one or the other would go outside and beckon the other by yellin': "Eee-Ahh-Kee" a couple of times. If the other was within earshot, he yelled the same thing back. Their call meant "Meet me half way" and the get together was on. We never used the Timmy call – we had our own made-up version and it worked just fine. When Jon would call out, we'd call back and then head for the fence. When either Chip or I did it - the process was reversed. We not only had some darn good bull sessions over the barbed wire fence but some serious plans were made there too. When I say serious plans, I mean such things as which field would make the best sleigh run if it snowed that night or which section of the woods was best when squirrel season opened in a day or two. It was always somethin' heavy duty like that and seldom just small talk. We were always deep thinkers and big planners back in those days. On school days 'long about dusk, way past time to head home, oftentimes we'd still be shootin' the breeze at the fence. Kinda' knee-deep in heavy conversation 'bout somethin' or other. Oftentimes, Jon's mother would yell for him to come home. On our side of the fence, Ma would ring the big black bell that stood on a post in the front yard. You could hear that ol' bell from 'bout anywhere within a mile or two and when we heard it – that meant come on home.

Jon was a noble lad of about 6 years old when we moved to the farm, which made him one year older than Chip and three years older than me. Age made no never-mind to us back then 'cause we all had the same interests and got along pretty good most of the time. The three of us boys sorta' grew up together. My brother and I always tried to be on our best behavior when we were around Jon's mother. Wasn't that she was uppity or better than us – nothin' like that – just didn't want that over-protective mother hen thinkin' we were a bad influence on Jon. After all, take him or leave him, he was the only friend we had to choose from within walkin' distance.

What used to get my dander up more than anything was every time she heard us makin' plans - no matter what – walkin' a quarter mile to the mailbox, headin' to the creek to catch tadpoles – you name it, there was one thing you could count on. And that one thing was her tellin' Jon he couldn't do it 'cause: "It wasn't safe". I got down-right sick and tired of hearin' that and so did he. After all – we figured it wasn't none of her Bees Wax what we done. In no time flat we made sure she wasn't within earshot durin' the plan makin' sessions. Our way of thinkin' was, "What a Mother don't know won't hurt her" and as a general rule we were right most of the time.

Bein' that Jon's mother was a school teacher and all, I'd bet ya two bits to the hole in a doughnut that she had a mighty early curfew on that old black and white T.V. set in their livin' room. So, at night while Chip and I were watchin' The Lone Ranger, Zorro or The Three Stooges, Jon had nothin' better to do than read a book or something goofy like that. Seemed like back then no matter what the subject of conversation, Jon could always talk over our head. Guess it was kinda' like the guy with book sense talkin' to the ignoramus. All that made no difference to us because whatever Jon said was the gospel – he knew everything. Thus was born the carved in stone our adage: "Jon Said...".

Jon seemed to know somethin' on just about any given topic. The boy never was prone to make-believe or tellin' down-right whoppers, but he was pretty good at sprinklin' in a little bull crap, here and there, kinda' like a chef spices up a good stew. Most of the time Jon would get off on a subject with the credibility of an encyclopedia. Neither of us boys ever "called" him on a story because we always figured he knew what he was talkin' about.

In an attempt to spread the wealth of knowledge, we'd quote him all the time, 'most always beginnin' with: "Jon said".

The "Jon said" thing did get a little old from time to time. Ma never paid too much attention to it but Dad did. Now and again, Dad would say somethin' and we'd correct him by sayin' somethin' like: "No way, Dad" or "That ain't right" and the very next words would be: "Jon said....". There was a few times when Dad got down-right pissed about it, sorta' like a dog does when a cat messes around with him once too often. My Dad was a man of wisdom and for him to be corrected by a 10 or 12 year old made him madder than a wet hen. Dad seldom argued the point but did mock us sayin': "Jon said, Jon said..." and then change the subject.

One other thing about Jon - not a day went by that he didn't finagle into a conversation his favorite word, "Evidently". The boy used that word every chance he got. Must have been his favorite word or somethin'. When the tree frogs started croakin', Jon would say: "Evidently, it's gunna' rain" or when the fish weren't bitin' he'd say: "Evidently, they ain't hungry". Evidently this and evidently that – everything was a matter of evidently.

Got to the point where when Chip made a comment to me about 'most anything, my one word response would be: "Evidently". Worked the other way around too. Every time I hear that word, I think of Jon.

Jon around 12 or 13 years old

Dad contemplating "But Dad, Jon Said..."

Fairfax Little League

Every Spring 'bout the time the daffodils start bloomin', out came the baseball mitts, bat and baseballs. Seemed everyone's blood started to flow about that time of year, sorta' like the sap in a maple tree. Gettin' rid of those winter coats, galoshes and the like was as welcome as the apple blossoms and the sound of the frogs down at the creek. Ma always called those frogs peepers. Makes a body try to relate with turtles and groundhogs and all the other creatures that been hibernatin' all winter. I guess me and the hibernatin' animals had somethin' in common.

Down the road about 12 miles or so - or maybe it was up the road 12 miles or so, not really sure on direction, was the town of Fairfax, Virginia. Fairfax city was about like comparin' New York City to Clifton when it came to stores and things to do. Fairfax had a hardware store, a new fangled barbershop with about three guys cuttin', new car dealers, a Peoples Drug Store and even had a McDonalds hamburger joint. I'm gunna' tell ya' somethin' right now - not too many people know. Brother Chip was on the Fairfax High School eighth grade football team and they had a

10:00 o'clock game one Saturday mornin' 'round the first of November. Ma had to get him there early for chalk talk and gettin' dressed, warm-ups and the like before the game so we got there around 8:30 or thereabouts. I didn't give a hoot about the game and the McDonalds right next door had their Grand Openin' that mornin'. A Grand Openin' meant they were openin' up for business for the very first time that very mornin'. My good friend David Petersen and I went to McDonalds rather than the game and stood in line for about two hours so we could be the very first customers. I bought a 15 cent hamburger around 11:00 a.m that day and was the very first customer they ever had. That McDonalds is still there today and I'm still their very first customer any way you shake it. Not many people know that little bit of history, but I do. Back then you could buy yourself a three course meal – a hamburger, French fries and a milk shake for 45 cents. That particular day I only had 15 cents on me. Made no difference whether I had 45 cents or only 15 – I was still their very first customer! I always figured the first customer thing was kinda' like an education – once you got it – they can't ever take it away from ya.

Fairfax was the county seat and had an old courthouse that was much the same then as it had been back in the old days. Rumor had it that John Mosby, better known as the "Gray Ghost", rode his horse up the stairs and into the building right smack-dab in the middle of the Civil War and kidnapped some big-shot Union guy. Truth is, he never actually did that, but did capture a Brigadier General and two Captains nearby the courthouse. No one knows how he and his boys got through heavy Union protection and pulled that off, but maybe that's why they called him the

"Gray Ghost" in the first place. So much for history, let's get back to baseball.

Ma got Chip hooked up in organized baseball sooner than me, mostly 'cause he was a year and a half older and better understood what was goin' on. I was about nine years old at the time and had the attention span of a Mexican Jumpin' Bean, so I wasn't quite ready for organized sports at that point. Fairfax Little League had two leagues – the majors and the minors. Chip was ten and playin' with the big boys in the majors and I was in the minors playin' for some team – the Cardinals, if memory serves me correctly.

The followin' year, Chip and I were on the same team in the major league. We played for the Rebels and Mr. Shahady was the coach. A year makes a big difference when a kid goes from 9 to 10 and by now, rather than payin' more attention to birds flyin' around, grasshoppers and cars goin' by, I was developin' into a real genuine baseball player. Chip could play 'bout any position on the field, short of catcher, but I played centerfield. Not braggin' - but not bad for my age. We had a pretty good team that year, 1958, but the next year was when we really came into bloom – I'm talkin' full blossom bloom - and I'm fixin' to tell ya all about it.

Fairfax Little League was organized baseball at it's best for Little Leaguers. The main stadium was right next to Fairfax High School and was a dandy. There were drop down dugouts with walls and a roof, a chain link fence down both first and third base lines, all the way to the outfield fence. The outfield fence was about five feet high consisting of advertisin' boards all the way from left to right field. Behind the center field part of the fence was a large score board. "Long about first base and third base were first class bleachers for the parents and rooters. Just beyond the first base bleachers was a full time snack bar and that snack bar had it all! They had sodas, hotdogs, potato chips and Bazooka bubble gum. Wasn't too much more a kid could ask for the way I saw it and there were times I couldn't wait for the game to end 'cause of it. The playin' field was limed off before every game, the pitcher had a mound and the grass was always cut. Now, that was a stadium!

There were three overflow ball fields not far away called Eaton Fields. Those fields weren't quite so fancy as Little League Stadium but were functional just the same.

After the 1958 season, the league was gettin' bigger and bigger. The big-shots decided it was time to move on up so here's what they did. They formed up two leagues with five teams each. There was the Eastern Division Majors and the Western Division Majors. Each league had five teams. Every team had a sponsor that anteed up enough money for the uniforms, bats, balls and all other necessary utensils. These weren't no junk uniforms either – they were the best money could buy. Ma let 'um know right up front that both of her boys had to be on the same team. She told 'um ain't no way she could drive 25 miles 'round trip one day for one and then 25 miles the next day for the other. Back then gasoline was around 25 cents a gallon and 'less she had her way, either we didn't play baseball at all, or you were talkin' serious money not countin' travelin' time. Ma won out.

Made sense to me – we weren't exactly within spittin' distance of the practice field or the stadium. They tell me there was some heavy "Wheelin' and Dealin'" and all kinds of "Horse Tradin'" goin' on for them Foley boys when the coaches went to choosin' players. The deal was a rotation pick – if ya know what I mean - one guy at a time - and it damn sure wasn't no "Eeenee-Meenee-Minee-Mo" ordeal. This was serious business. I guess our coach had to pick two and then skip a round or offer up his wife up to run the snack bar or somethin' like that to get us both. Ya see, the deal was, Chip was considered a superstar the year before and everybody wanted him. I wasn't all that bad a baseball player, but still the tagalong - kinda' like when ya go to buy somethin' that ya really want and they won't sell it to you, 'less ya take somethin' else with it. Maybe that's how the coach got two for one in the first place. Ma's demand put the coaches in a real mess. Never did hear the particulars on the dealin's, but Chip and I ended up on the Melpar Chiefs with Captain Wells for our coach. The coach was called "Captain" 'cause he was a Captain in rank on the Fairfax County police department. You'd of never figured him to be a cop – he was just too nice a guy. We had practice about three times a week for a month and a half or so before the season started. Captain Wells' son, Butch, was on the team and even though he was a first baseman, he was second string 'cause brother Chip was the best first baseman Fairfax Little League ever saw. They probably ain't never seen the likes of him since. At twelve years old, Chip played first like them guys in the pros. When an infield hit was thrown to first, he'd have his left foot on the bag and stretch out like a rubber band to save a quarter second on the play. Ain't no tellin' how many guys got called "Out", that normally would'a been safe with the same hit against any other team.

I was a year younger than Chip, but came along pretty quick and next thing ya know I was that pig's ear that came with the silk purse, or however that expression goes. Like I said, Chip could play 'most any position and when he wasn't playin' first base he was our star pitcher. The boy was the fastest pitcher in either league. He had a mean fastball and when that thing was headin' down the pike, there wasn't none too much time for decision makin' by the batter - and I ain't just "Whistling Dixie" either. The boy pitched a good many of our games that year and ended up strikin' out 94 guys in 58 innings. Rounded off, that's better than one and a half guys an inning. Now, on the flip side – he did hit 7 batters with the ball. The boy threw the ball so hard and fast that when he hit um' with a pitch - they were either gone for the game or gone for the season! Chip just never did anything half-hearted – it was all or nothin'. I *never* even wanted him to pitch to me in battin' practice! We ended up winnin' 12 games that year and comin' in second 8 times. Both of us made the "All Star Team".

Most of the teams in our division were no-'count, but our arch rival was Jim Scott's "Rebels". Coach Scott was ruthless on those kids and if they didn't win, he made their life miserable. The Little Bucs and the White Sox beat us once in a while but to lose to the Rebels was a fate worse than death. When we won, I went nuts and when we lost I was pissed. Dad always told me back then: "Win like you're used to it and lose like you enjoy it". I ain't sure Dad knew how much was on the line when givin' that kind of advice. After all, winnin' was "Braggin' Rights". Never understood Dad's preachin' at the time, but later in life what he said did make sense.

When the Chiefs and the Rebels played, the stadium was packed. All the Moms and Dads were there, little sisters and brothers, big sisters and brothers, aunts, uncles, friends, neighbors - you name it! If ya ever read that poem "Casey at the Bat", well, Fairfax Little League stadium had a strange likin' to "Mudville" for those games. Those games were like two gladiators in the coliseum – only one was goin' to win and each of us wanted to win about as much as them two gladiators, if you get the picture.

In one particular game the Rebels star pitcher, Dave Penny, was on the mound. Late in the game I hit an "In the Park" home run to win the game. An in the park home run was when you got a good hit and somehow made it all the way around the bases and scored without gettin' out. Those things were rare especially against a good team like the Rebels. That happened when I was 11 and Chip was still on the team, age limit for Little League was 12.

The next year we won the "Pennant", which meant first place in the division. That year one of my best friends, Donny Stoops, was pitchin' for the Rebels (His real name was Donny, but I always called him "Poopsie"). Anyway, Donny had a fastball ya almost couldn't see. That game was what ya might call, "Real Braggin' Rights", 'cause of bein' so late in the season. Even though we were best of friends, Donny woulda' rather hit me in the head with the ball and knocked me out - than lose that game. 'Long about the fifth inning I came up to bat and Donny was throwin' like a mad man – had this particular thing for me - the boy wanted me out bad. About the third pitch the ball not only went over the center field fence but over the scoreboard to boot. By the time I was 12 that, "Win like you're used to it" thing was startin' to settle in. I never said one single word to Donny about that home run shot or winnin' the game!

When it comes to braggin' about home runs, let me get back to Chip for a minute. I don't remember how many home runs he hit, but I can tell ya one thing – when he hit 'um, they weren't no love taps. We were playin' at Little League Stadium one day and Chip was at bat. The pitcher wound up and threw the ball right down the pike. Chip hit that damn ball so hard and so far I doubt they ever found it. I always figured the best place to start lookin' for the ball was the next county over. That ball went down the left field line like it was shot out of a rifle – only one problem – the ball was about one foot on the wrong side of the foul pole. Chip ended the season with 32 hits and 61 at bats for an unbelievable battin' average of .525. I was 24 hits with 60 at bats addin' up to a .400 battin' average, which ain't bad either.

The followin' year, 1960, the Chiefs won the pennant and I was selected by the league coaches to the "All Star Team" for the second straight year. Chip had moved on to "Babe Ruth League" for 13 to 15 year old boys and left me behind on my own. That year I was second in the league with a 492 battin' average.

You might have your opinion about what was goin' on back then - and you can say whatever you want to say - and that's just fine with me – *but,* in my opinion, and I was there witnessin' the whole thing - Chip was the best damn baseball player I ever saw when we were kids – and that's sayin' somethin', by crackie!

If'n he hadn't got distracted by girls or whatever - I do believe the boy might'a played for the Washington Senators or the New York Yankees or somebody like that !

Fairfax Little League - August 1960 - Me

Fairfax Little League - August 1960 - Chip

Me at bat during the Fairfax Little League All-Star game
with the Vienna Little League All-Stars

Learn't How to Cuss from Chip

As I told you a while ago, I got two hogs for my third birthday which was the day after we moved to the farm. Those hogs were so much fun Mom and Dad decided to get a couple more. The only bad thing about the hogs was when I had to "Slop 'Um". Slop 'um is hog talk for feedin' 'um. The good part was when they'd take a notion to get out of the pen. Ma would tell us boys to 'round 'um up and get 'um back in the pen. We didn't mind that at all and took our good old fashioned time doin' it. We were kinda' little back in those days and in our half-hearted attempt to get the hogs back in the pen, we would hop on their backs and ride around for a while. That was fun for us and the hogs didn't seem to mind it either. After we had gotten ourselves plenty dirty and stinkin' too, we'd head 'um on into the pen and look around for somethin' else equally as fun to do. Only problem was – that Hog Ridin' was a hard act to follow.

City folks just don't understand a country boys idea of fun – ya see, there's not a lot to do for a kid on a farm 'less you create your own entertainment. Entertainment of the simplest kind will do just fine most of the time for country boys. Like the time Chip and I made us a genuine telephone. We got two old tin cans and poked a small hole in the bottom of each. Next we got a piece of string about a hundred feet long. Feed the string through the hole on each can and tied a knot big enough that the string couldn't pull back through. He got one can and I got the other. We paced off a hundred feet and pulled the string taunt. Chip spoke into his can while I had mine to my ear and then it went vise versa. We had a good telephone conversation that day and as I recall it went somethin' like: "Can ya hear me" then "Yea, I can hear you, can you hear me?". That phone system really did work good, but I'm not at all sure a body coulda' called long distance on it. Best part of the whole thing was - you could talk as long as you wanted to with no party line interruptions.

Gettin' back to the livestock. I was just a young'un back then and I can't remember the exact sequence of the animals comin' and goin'. Seems to me after Anna and Hetty came along, there was a couple of ducks, a few chickens and then Abigail the cow. Ol' Abigail belonged to my oldest sister Karen. I got no recollection how that cow came to bein' hers and after talkin' to Karen the other day, neither does she. Anyway the cow was hers. After Abigail came a Hertford cow we named Laura Lee and Charlie the bull. Laura Lee was just another cow but Charlie was a real bull. Charlie had a bad attitude and it was best not to take your eye off him if'n you were in the barnyard. Charlie liked to charge you like you were a matador with a red cape. We could usually side step him, long as we had a little lead time, and slip through the fence to safety. Chip and I used to wrestle in the barn among the hay bales and that was a heap of fun. Just about every time one of us would lose his baseball cap and the other would quickly grab it and pitch it over the fence into Charlie's pen. That was always hilarious for the guy doin' the throwin'.

One day, Charlie decided he needed to get out of the barnyard and over into the field with the Momma cows. He knocked the top board off the fence and figured he could jump over the second and bottom boards. Didn't work. Ol' Charlie only made it two thirds the way and got himself hung up in an awful kinda' way. The more he struggled, the worse it got. I had a mishap on a fence one time and I knew just how he felt. I told Mr. Porter about the incident and asked him why the bull acted so crazy. He told me that's just the way bulls do and that sometimes grown men act like bulls and get themselves tangled-up in worse predicaments than that fence and that someday I'd understand.

In time, we got a few more cows but this time they were black angus. Charlie didn't give a hoot what the cows looked like and when love called he was there. Each year a cow or two would have a calf. The little males were converted into steers and raised a couple of years then sent to the slaughterhouse in Manassas. We didn't have any Bye, Byes, Grand Farewells or Last Rights for the steers goin' to slaughter, we just went over to Manassas a week or so later and picked up the freezer wrapped steaks and put 'um in the freezer at home. Those were the best steaks in the world and we always kept a low profile on talkin' about last night's dinner when we were around the Momma cows.

Karen claims that one of her chores was to feed the cows and she was right to a certain degree. There was always a 55 gallon metal barrel full of molasses flavored corn grain in the barn and a wooden trough out behind the barn. Karen's job was to fill a bucket full of grain and put it in the trough. When it came to bustin' up a bale of hay and throwin' it over the fence for the cows, Karen was a girl, so that part of the job was handled by either Chip or me. None of us minded feedin' the cows 'cause that was one of our designated chores on the farm and you did it every day without bein' reminded that it needed doin'. That was every day, mind ya' – rain, snow, sleet or hail. None of us needed no remindin' when it came to farm chores, after all, that's what that twenty five cent allowance every week was all about.

One of my jobs or chores was waterin' the cows. Down below the last out-shed by the chicken house was an old porcelain bathtub we used for waterin' the heifers and Charlie too. We had runnin' water to the tub with one of those old time hand-drawn spigots. Gettin' water to the cows was pretty easy in the spring, summer and fall, but in the winter it was a bitch. Reason was – the water in the tub froze up and so did the spigot. Before school, I had to bust the frozen water and get the ice out of the tub and then hand carry buckets of water down to the tub – hopin' the cows would take a swig or two before it froze up again. By the time I got home from school, the whole thing started over again. Thank the Dear Lord, winter only lasted three months – four on the bad years. Made no difference whether it was a sun shiny day or there was three feet of snow on the ground – the cows needed waterin' and I was the water boy.

'Long side the porcelain waterin' tub was a pretty decent sized peach tree standin' there all by itself. For the cows it was a good shade tree in the summer and served as a scratchin' post when they had a hankerin' – mostly when the flies were powerful bad. Those cows rubbed the bark on that tree plumb shiny as a new dime. When the tree decided to grow some peaches as it did most every year, the cows would reach up and pick 'um off the tree or just wait 'til they fell to the ground. Ate a few peaches off that tree myself before the cows got to 'um. The ol' cows always liked me climbin' that tree to get to the good ones due to the fact that I shaked a few of the mediocre ones to the ground in doin' it.

There's a difference 'tween cows and dogs. A dog will eat just about anything and if it happens to have bones in it, he eats it bones and all. A cow eats grass, and the like, and then chews his cud. The way that works is the cow will eat somethin' and then regurgitate it and keep on chewin' on it and that's what ya call the cud. Seen many a cow stand there for hours on end chewin' the same cud - kinda' like a guy does when he's chawin' tobacco. Only difference was – cows don't spit while chewin' their cud. Well, the peaches had seeds, so now what's a cow supposed to do? Those ol' cows ate the peaches and spit the seeds out like a person does when he's eatin' watermelon. That was one of the coolest things I ever saw at the farm. Mr. Porter claimed a cow had better sense than a dog and that's why they spit the seeds out. I didn't have the heart to tell Duffy about that claim - matter of fact I never told anyone that – 'til now.

I reckon everybody has one of those days, now and again, where ya just don't feel like gettin' out of bed in the mornin'. 'Specially when it's either cold or rainy. Seemed like every time one of those days would roll around, Ma would come to our room real early in the mornin' and say: "Boys, get up – the cows are out". They always say that the grass is greener on the other side of the fence, and I guess that's the way the cows seen it too on cold rainy mornin's. Seems they'd always find the weakest board or two on the fence and knock 'um off the post just good enough to get out. Chip and I were up, dressed and out the door in no time flat headin' for wherever the cows were. I handled those situations kinda' with the mind-set of a border collie but Chip never liked the "Cow's out" thing even a little bit. Many a mornin' I'd watch him runnin' across the field cussin' like a sailor at them cows. When he got within range he always threw rocks at them either in an attempt to head 'um on home or teach them a lesson – mostly teach 'um a lesson I think. Chip cussed at the cows the whole time. Went somethin' like: "Blankity, blankity, blank you blankity, blank cows". His sentences were always short and to the point and damn sure weren't anything he used around the house. He was cussin' those dumb animals before he got to where they were and then all the way back to the barnyard. Along with his cussin' the cows, he wasn't none to sparin'with the rock throwin'. After we got 'um back in we had to fix the fence where they got out. Chip was still cussin' the cows while poundin' the nails. I learn't 'bout every cuss word I know from brother Chip.

Horses Ain't all the Same

'Long about age 10, Mom and Dad found a guy named Mr. Namey in Tyson's Corner, Virginia who had some horses and gave horseback ridin' lessons. Tyson's Corner was like Chantilly – a one stop light crossroads with a vegetable stand on one corner. They took us kids over there a couple of times and he taught us how to ride a horse. The guy was a little short and abrupt personality-wise, but that was O.K. with me – all I wanted to do was learn how to ride a horse. We already had one horse on the farm, a handsome quarter horse by the name of Babe. Shortly after learnin' how to ride, Mom and Dad got three more horses named Blaze, Lady and Crackerjack.

Babe was the family's horse, Blaze, a brown and white two tone belonged to Chip, Lady, a black and white paint was mine and Crackerjack, an ol' gray swayback nag belonged to Kevin. Crackerjack had the cribbin' disease which caused him to go around gnawin' on fence boards all the time. Made no sense to me why the nag had to be chewin' up all the fence boards and makin' belchin' sounds all the time, but that's what he done and seemed content doin' it.

Horses are as different from each other as people are from one to the next. Somethin' like girls – just 'cause they're pretty – don't mean they got good sense. You'd think, horses bein' horses and all, they'd all be the same – ain't no way. They're as different as a polecat and a mockin'bird! Speaking of mockin'birds, I asked Mr. Porter one time how a mockin'bird could sing so many songs and then act nuttier than a fruit cake. He told me some people call 'um a mockin'bird and some people call 'um a catbird 'cause of the way they sing a pretty song one minute - then the next minute - two of 'um would tag-team together dive bombin' a cat or a dog from the blind side – bein'more strategic and aggravatin' and than a horse fly. He told me a mockin'bird was Mother Nature formin' a kinship 'tween a rosebud and a polecat. One minute she was beautiful and the next minute she stunk. I had to think on that for a while but it did kinda' make sense, time I thought it through.

My horse, Lady, didn't like to be ridden or somethin'. If she did, she was kinda' like some girls I had known – she liked to play hard to get. I had to corner her up to where she couldn't run off to put the bridle on her. Once that was done she was gentle as a lamb and as obedient as a good housedog. That behavior applies to some girls too. We never used saddles too much back then – just bridle 'um up, jump on bareback and take off. I took Lady everywhere. But then, maybe in her opinion, she took me. That's another one of them things that all depends on where you're sittin' or standin' I guess. We covered every crack and cranny of our farm and went all back across the Elgin farm and even back to see Marshall and Nelly many a time. You could ride horses down the paved roads back then due to not much traffic and all, and I even rode her up to See Mr. Porter now and again. Lady was a sweet girl and I had a special thing for her. She was just different – she never brushed me off and never flirted with any other boys. There was a love made in Heaven, or the barnyard, all dependin' on how you wanted to look at it

Chip's horse, Blaze, was great at first but the less he got rode, the less he wanted to be rode. Got to the point where he was about as obedient as a grasshopper. He was somethin' like some people I've known – give 'um an inch and next thing ya know they want the ruler. Blaze was faster than greased lightnin'. We'd take him down to the far end of the field that joined the barnyard where the barn was that didn't have a door and was always open. When ya turned him around, he'd make a beeline for the barn and ya better be hangin' on good 'cause he was in fourth gear in about three steps. When he hit the barnyard he slowed down just a tad but was still movin' pretty fast when he went straight into the barn and stopped on a dime. Problem was – the barn door was a lot lower than your head and if ya didn't duck, you were in some serious Poo Poo. Blaze knew what he was doin' and probably thought it was funny knowin' that, sooner or later, he'd fine a sucker and knock his head plumb off. If you were ridin' him for the first time, he'd break ya in real fast of ever wantin' to get on a horse again.

Crackerjack was dumber than a brick and about as set in his ways as a 17 year locust. He was an old swayback nag that I think Mr. Namey took advantage of a situation with

- when it came to sellin' him for good money to a couple of folks who weren't exactly what you'd call experienced horse traders. Crackerjack was a good ol' nag and he'd do anything ya wanted him to do and never seemed to question authority. He was the one I was tellin' ya about a while ago that like to gnaw on fence boards so when it came to bridlin' him up, all ya had to do was go to where he was gnawin'. Ol' Crackerjack was about as docile as a Japanese beetle and a loveable ol' bag of bones too. When ya bridled him up he would gladly take ya anywhere ya wanted to go and he was pretty dog-gone fast on his feet too, though you'd never have guessed it by lookin' at him.

We had some real good friends, Bunny and Larry Jeblick that lived down the road a ways almost to the Clifton Corporate Limit sign goin' into the village. Bunny was Kevin and Chip's age and Larry was my age. Larry was my best friend at school and Bunny was the heartthrob of every boy at Clifton elementary, includin' Chip. Bunny was prettier than Annette Funicello on the Mickey Mouse Club show and could have had the pick of the litter when it came to all those "Rag Muppin'" boys at school. She knew it too, and handled it pretty good. They were big into horse-back ridin' too and we would get together every now and again and ride as a group. I wasn't too much into the group-ridin' thing and always had to ride ahead like the scout in an Old West T.V. show.

Not that I was all that independent, but I had a thing about just walkin' the horses down the road as opposed to haulin' ass wherever I went. When I was on horseback, it was all business just like ya see on T.V. in them old time westerns.

When we rode like that, with girls and all, the girls always had their horses decked out with saddles. I never was too much on the saddle thing 'cause if you weren't careful when you were tightenin' up the girth belt, the horse would reach around and nip ya. They usually got ya in the side just above the belt and if you ever been nipped by a horse, you know just how bad that hurts. Another reason I didn't like saddles was 'cause the horse didn't like them either. After ya put the saddle blanket on and then threw up the saddle and were fastenin' the girth belt, ya had to be real careful that the horse didn't bloat his stomach to compensate for a tight belt. Bein' a rational kinda' guy, I did understand the girth strap, from the horse's point of view, however, when he let the bloat out the belt was loose and when ya went to get on, the saddle would slide around under the horse and that was a real mess. It was always a whole lot simpler to just ride bareback for both me and the horse.

When the Bowman's moved off their farm into the city, they had to do some scalin' down. I told you about ol' Smokey the red bone hound and where he ended up, but they also had their oldest daughter, Linda's horse to get rid of too. Our farm was the ideal place. Mom and Dad loved Uncle Moir and Aunt Gen so much that they'd of helped 'um out with anything includin' their three boys if necessary. Kenny, Robby and Mark were Hellions from the get go – good boys but a little on the wild side - and I'm sure there was many a time Moir and Gen wished they'd made a package deal out of the whole thing.

Some of the most fun times at the farm were when the Bowman's came to visit. The boys were farm boys turned city slicker and always had some cool stuff to show us or tell about. Like the time they taught us how to make homemade missiles. It wasn't any more than fillin' an empty CO_2 cartridge full of match heads and putting a tiny fuse at the base where we stuffed the match heads in. When we set that thing on an elevated rock or some kind of incline and lit it – all Hell broke loose. That missile took off with a trail of smoke so fast you couldn't hardly see it. After they were gone, Chip and I got a bunch of empty CO_2's and made us a mess of them rockets. If one of those things had ever flipped around, like fire works do sometimes, it would have gone plumb through ya. I guess when it came to ice skatin' and homemade rockets, we had a certain degree of luck with us. Those guys were more fun than a barrel of monkeys and always had a bunch of funny stories to share.

After the Bowman's moved off their farm, Linda, their oldest daughter, would come out to our farm once in a while to ride her horse, Snowball, that we were storin' for 'um. I'd always ride Lady right along with her. Linda was six or seven years older than me and pretty as a picture. I guess ya might say I had a crush on her or somethin' like that. Seemed every time I took a gander at that girl my heart started poundin' like a grouse drummin'.

As ol' Snowball started gettin' up in years, and her ridin' days were done, she just kinda' hung around the barnyard and fields puttin' in her last days. She was a lovable old thing. One day she went down and just couldn't get back up. Couldn't have picked a worse day of the year for doin' that either. It was about zero degrees outside and started to snow. By nightfall the snow was gettin' pretty deep and still comin'. The wind was howlin', the snow was accumulatin' - it was gettin' colder and colder and there was no sign of it lettin' up. We carried some hay bales down to where she was layin' in the field and tried to build up a wall to ease the wind and blindin' snow. We cared for her as best we could, well into the night. Next mornin' she was dead. It ain't so bad that ya gotta' go, 'cause we all gotta' go at some point in time, but the night she cashed in was just the down-right worst anybody could'a ever picked.

Every kid should get in some horseback ridin' if he gets a chance. I highly recommend that over just sittin' around the house all day sorryin' away.

Kevin, Chip, Jon and Me (foreground) with Duffy in the background (February 1956)

Mike left - Chip right (around 1953)

Me riding Lady June 1958

A riding expedition with the girls

Kevin

Chip

Marshall and Nelly

I was tellin' ya a while ago about the dirt road that went on past the dump a mile or so and ended up at Bull Run. Well, back there in the middle of nowhere was an old wooden house where Marshall and Nelly Davis lived. The house was plenty old and Marshall told me the Yankees burnt half of it down durin' the Civil War. Don't know that to be fact, but that's what he said. Might very well have been true since there was an old Civil War trench on the crest of a ridge where the river took a right sharp bend 'bout a half mile upstream and another one about a mile, as the crow flies, down river where Occoquan and Wolf Run meet up. Found the down stream trench one day while squirrel huntin' over on the Elgin farm. There were barbed wire fences back in those days 'tween the farms but really no such thing as trespassin' on other people's property, 'cause nobody seemed to pay it much mind. A kid could do a lot of things back in the 50's that would probably land him in the pokey years later. Like the time Jon and Chip and I hooked up his old aluminum boat to his Dad's tractor and drove it back through the woods to the Run. The "Run" is what we called Bull Run. We put the thing in the water and headed on downstream with our fishin' stuff, two 22 rifles and a handgun. When we'd 'round a bend in the river you could always count on a log in the water with a half dozen skill pots on it. A skill pot was what we called them water turtles with a flat shell and a red ring around the outside of the shell. We'd cut the motor, take aim and on the count of three, cut loose on the turtles. It was hard to keep track of a hit or a miss due to all of the turtles slidin' off the log and into the water at the sound of the shots. That was a lot of fun but I sure wouldn't try somethin' like that today. Anyway....

That house was for sure was another one of those houses where you never got past the kitchen. There was no electricity back there and no runnin' water either. Never saw too many candles on a visit, so I ain't rightly sure how they handled the light situation after dark. Marshall claimed they didn't need no runnin' water, 'cause Nelly could run down over the hill to the branch and fetch a bucket of water faster than you could draw one out of a tap. The outhouse was only a few feet from the kitchen door and neither it nor the house looked like they'd ever made acquaintance with a paint brush. The kitchen had a table, three chairs and a four-burner wood stove. That stove burned year 'round due to that's how they fixed their meals, 'bout like the Porter's done. There was a couple of pegs in the wall for coat hangin' in the winter or whatever you wanted to hang on 'um in the summer. The few windows in the house were those big ol' four-pane kind and were so old they always had a frosty look to 'um even in the summer. Didn't look to me like the windows had been washed in the last fifty years or so. They only had two of those windows in the kitchen, one on each side of the room and they usually had stuff piled here and there to the point where you couldn't see out even if they had been clean. There was an old wooden door off the kitchen leadin' to the upstairs. That door was always closed.

Marshall and Nelly raised some mighty fine vegetables back there in the fields. He didn't have a tractor or modern plow. All his cultivatin' was with an old horse pullin' an ancient hand maneuvered wooden handled plow. Marshall would come out sellin' his produce in the summer and even though we had our own garden, we always bought some of his. They grew peanuts back there too. 'Round Christmas time every year I'd make a point to go visit - knowin' they'd always offer up some of their homegrown and home fixed chocolate covered peanuts. Don't think I've ever ate nothin' so good in all my born days.

They always raised about an acre of sweet corn right next to their house. One thing 'bout sweet corn - it drives them raccoons plumb crazy and they just can't stay out'a the patch. That ain't good when you are growin' it to either eat or sell and the sellin' of it is about your only income. You ain't gunna' believe how they kept the coons out of the patch. The field sloped on down away from the house and Marshall would stay up half the night, settin' on an old crate with a bucket full of rocks by his side. When he heard a coon down over the hill thrashin' around, he'd throw a rock down in the corn and the scared coon would take off figurin' somebody was on to him. 'Long about the middle of the night Nelly would relieve him 'til sun up. That ain't exactly what I'd call scientific corn raisin', but it worked.

When we gave away them four redbone hounds, Dad gave the best of the bunch, Smokey, to his dear friend Moir Bowman who owned a farm off of Pope's Head road not far from Fairfax city. The Government built a Niki Site right next to his farm and due to how close it was made him sell the farm off to the government. Uncle Moir, as we called him (Not really no kin) gave the hound to a guy he knew and moved to a subdivision in Falls Church. Uncle Moir was the about the kindest and most givin' person I've ever known. He was definitely my favorite of all of Dad's friends and Dad had some good ones. One day he decided to go see how Smokey was doin'. The guy he gave him up to wasn't home and Smokey was tied to a tree 'bout starved to death - ribs showin', ears droopin', sad eyed and near dead. 'Peared to him the poor dog hadn't had food or water in a week or better. Uncle Moir cut the rope, put the poor wretch in his car and took him on home. When he had Smokey half way back to normal, he called Dad, told him the story and asked if he knew of a good home for the dog. Dad said he knew just the guy who'd take care of him real good. Marshall and Nelly jumped all over the chance to have 'umselves a good dog and back there is where ol' Smokey lived out the rest of his life. Smokey didn't need no luxury – a doghouse and food on a regular basis was his idea of "High Cotton" and by crackie - he had just that.

Wasn't a coon, possum or groundhog safe within a mile of the house when Smoky was on the prowl. Marshall claimed that ol' Smokey once killed a 30 pound coon. Bein's that even a jumbo coon only gets up to about 10 or 15 pounds, I just figured Marshall didn't know the difference between 10 and 30 and he was tryin' to let me know that it was a mighty big 'un.

The road back to Marshall and Nelly's house was through the woods a right good ways and then opened up into about 15 acres of fields. There was a gradual grade down to the house 'bout a hundred yards or so after you came out of the woods. Looked the same every time we went back there – a decrepit old house with smoke comin' out of the chimney - spring, summer, fall or winter, made no difference what time of year. Hadn't been for the smoke, a body would of figured he's come on somethin' out of a fiction book, somethin' abandoned or somethin' lost in time. But, that's just how them folks lived and bein's ya can't miss somethin' you never had or even knew about, they were content. When we were about a hundred paces or so from the clearin', ol' Smokey started bellerin'. The ol' boy was so sharp he either smelt us or heard us long before we made our presence. I always say: "If ya never heard a good redbone beller - than ya ain't never heard good country music". Still believe that to this day.

Marshall was a good-sized man with a moon face, every other tooth missin' and a vocabulary of a couple of hundred words at best. Looked to me like he never changed his coveralls and when he was around, you were best off standin' up-wind. Couldn't read or write and never went to school a day in his life. On the other hand, Nelly had a little learnin' to her and could at least read and write. She was a small woman with a screechy country voice and a word count considerably more than Marshall. When she spoke it was direct and to the point without an overabundance of adjectives. When I say direct, I don't mean abrupt - just to the point and she 'most always smiled when she was talkin'. The way I knew she had some learnin' to her was – we never got any letters or nothin' like that from her, but she was always good for a Christmas card every year – she walked out and hand placed the card in our mailbox with no postage stamp on it. Nelly was into recyclin' before anybody ever heard tell of it. On her Christmas cards, you could always see where she'd erased somebody else's name off one she got the year before and wrote her own name on it and Marshall's to. That ain't bein' cheap, that's just down-right frugal the way I saw it and like Mr. Porter told me one time: "It ain't the givin' that counts - it's the thought behind it".

Nelly was a little ol' "Raggedy Ann" lookin' woman who was mighty country-like in her talkin' but she did always have somethin' pleasant to say. I never was too good at peggin' a guys age back then, but Nelly told me once that she'd lived in that old house for 65 years. I reckon, most likely she was born there. Nelly was mighty comfortable in her country-livin' life style.

One day she came out to the highway - as she called that two lane rural country road - and stopped by our house for a visit. Her visit wasn't too long after we got our very first black and white T.V. set. Nelly said she'd never heard tell of a T.V. set before. When we showed her how it worked, she stood her distance with her eyes 'bout bugged out of her head. She couldn't believe the movin' pictures or that people were talkin' out of that box like they were right there in the room. She'd probably heard a radio before but the T.V. was far beyond her feeble imagination.

Another day Marshall came to the house and told us: "Nelly done broke her leg". We called the Clifton Voluntary Fire Department and told 'um 'bout the situation. They sent their one ambulance out to pick her up and take her to the doctor. The ambulance meandered through the woods, down past the dump and on back to where the house was. They didn't have the siren blastin' but did have the red and white flashin' lights on. Nelly'd never seen a car or truck more than one color before in her whole life and when she seen that red and white thing comin' with the flashin' lights on it in the daytime - she hopped, skipped, jumped and crawled her way across the field and into the woods to get away from it. She'd never seen nothin' like it and was scared 'bout half to death, figurin' it was somethin' comin' from outer space. "Less you saw it first hand, it's mighty hard to relate to their back-woods way of thinkin', livin' and doin' things.

Now if I'm gunna' tell ya the truth and the whole truth 'bout them folks - there was actually three people livin' in that old house. There was Marshall and Nelly as I told ya, and there was also Aunt Elsie. Have no idea what kin she was to 'um. Aunt Elsie was older than either Marshall or Nelly and in appearance had a strikin' resemblance to a human "Scare-a-Crow". She was a skinny ol' rag-muppin' lookin' thing - dressed in homemade clothes with sunkin' eyes, wire-rim glasses and a corn cob pipe. Her hair was gray and pulled back under a straw hat and she was always sittin' in the far corner of the kitchen out of the way of things. She was about the damnedest lookin' excuse of a human bein' I'd ever seen. Have no idea whether or not she could talk 'cause every time I ever went callin', she never so much as uttered one single word. Don't know if she even could talk. She did smile every now and again and her teeth were 'bout like Marshall's – better than half of 'um missin'. I'd wager that 'tween the two of 'um, they didn't have a full set total, but that's only guessin'.   In all the times I ever went to see 'um, she was always sittin' in the same place. I never once saw her stand up or move from that chair or that spot.

In the later years at the farm when I went a callin', Elsie wasn't in the kitchen no more. Neither Marshall or Nelly ever said nothin' as to her whereabouts - and I never asked. If anybody'd wanted to lay a little wager - I'd a put my money on she up and died one day and when she did they took her over in the woods somewhere and dug a hole. Marshall and Nelly were good people.

Christmas at the Farm

The first week of September each year brought the return to school and the first of the annual huntin' seasons – Dove season. School startin' back was pretty cool – seein' all your good friends that you hadn't seen since last June. After the first two or three days you'd done showed off all your new clothes so by the second week everything was back to normal and usually just as borin' as the year before.

Dove season was the same as school but different in a way. I couldn't wait to get back out in the fields lookin' around. Ya had the same terrain and the same corn fields to hunt this year as last alright, but where the birds were plentiful last year – there wasn't a single one this year and of course that went vice versa all dependin' on the fields and the birds. School was pretty much the same, in that you had the same terrain and same classrooms as last year, but where the pretty girls had been the year before there weren't too many this year, 'cause either they'd all flown off to middle school or what was left wasn't much worth messin' with. On the other hand where the ugly girls had been the year before, well, some of 'um had changed over the summer and weren't so bad this year. Sometimes, I felt like girls and doves had a lot in common.

About the time the girls and the doves were gettin' to be about as boring as last week's news, along came October 1st - the openin' day of squirrel season. That was always my favorite time of the year, 'cause by then you pretty much had your eye on one girl, which gave you a reason to even go to school and when ya got home there was somethin' to look forward to also. As soon as I got off the bus I'd throw my books and homework down on the kitchen table, grab my single shot 20 gauge shotgun and head for the woods. The leaves were beginnin' to change color and the woods were as pretty as a bluegill hittin' a poppin' bug. I always liked the Hickory trees best. The leaves were as yellow as a full moon and the squirrels were always in 'um. Most any squirrel hunter will agree that Hickory trees were best for squirrels "cause you could hear 'um barkin' or cuttin' the nuts or shakin' a branch. Squirrels don't migrate like doves but some sections of the woods were better huntin' this year than they were the year before. Squirrels were more predictable than doves. All ya had to do was find yourself a good hickory or beech tree and set down on a log and wait. Made no difference where their nests were, they'd always come back to the same feedin' trees. You could stand in a cornfield for hours on end waitin' for a dove to fly over and when they did, you never had the same shot twice. Doves were just as unpredictable as girls. One would come by you "Hell Bent for Election" or in other words, so fast she was gone before you could get a shot off. The next would fly by slow as a leaf fallin' off a tree. They'd fly by erratic like a grouse or glide like a buzzard soakin' up a September afternoon. Dove huntin' ain't for beginners, but for that matter, neither are girls.

'Long about November we started plannin' for Thanksgiving and began snoopin' around for this year's Christmas tree. Things were different back in the 50's. For example, there was no such thing as a store bought Christmas tree or expensive presents. Back then you found yourself a nice shaped pine tree and chopped it down, took it home and put it up. One year Chip and I took off on Dads tractor with the trailer taggin' along one Saturday mornin' lookin' for a tree. Chip being older and all, figured he had to do the drivin' of the tractor - and that was fine with me. It was overcast and colder than an ice cube that day, but when you're young and it was somethin' as important as goin' to find yourself a Christmas tree, ya didn't really pay no mind to the temperature. Chip drove the tractor down the road toward the Elgin farm and maneuvered it real good down Doug Hill, which was so long and steep it wasn't fit for much more than a Mountain Goat. We went on down past Wolfe Run and up the next ridge toward the Davis' general store. Chip felt like he was "Dad" or somethin' when drivin' the tractor and I just held on like I normally did. Had it in his mind he was a "Big Cheese" when drivin' that thing. Made no difference to me, I was on a mission lookin' for a Christmas tree. We turned into "Lakewood Estates" about two miles down the road on the left and started lookin' hard for a tree. Lakewood Estates was a place where some guy bought up a patch of land and put in a paved road back to a lake. The guy subdivided the property off into lots and was tryin' to sell 'um. Been there for two or three years and hadn't sold a one as best I recall. Anyway, we stopped the tractor and took off on foot lookin' for a tree. We finally found one, chopped it down, put it on the trailer and headed on home. Don't remember ever goin' that far huntin' for a tree in my whole life, but we did get a good one that year.

Many of our Christmas presents were inexpensive or even sometimes used. Made no difference – Christmas was fun back then before they went and commercialized it. Both Ma and sister Karen were awful good cooks so through the Christmas holidays we ate pretty high on the hog. Ham, turkey, cookies, candy, fruit cake, you name it – we had it. Every year there was Christmas gatherin's at school and church. At school it was mostly singin' Christmas carols, wishin' everybody a Merry Christmas, eatin' cookies and stuff like that. At church it was toned down a bit and focused on what Christmas was really all about. The Christmas carols were the religious ones like "The First Noel" and Oh, Holy Night. We needed that part of Christmas too, I always figured 'cause that part of Christmas don't happen too much these days. Over the years we've kinda' lost connection with a real genuine Country Christmas and the true meanin' of Christmas. And for that I'm a bit saddened.

Before Mom and Dad started renovatin' the farmhouse, the walls were plaster and in many places the plaster had fallen off the walls or ceiling leavin' sight of the lath strips and beams. We never paid that any mind back then – we were a happy and lovin' family and that's all that mattered. We always put the tree in the same place, right next to the old non-functional brick chimney in the livin' room. Decoratin' the tree was about as much fun as a kid could have. Dad would usually do the lights and us kids did the rest. After that was done, Dad and Chip would install the oval tracks for old Lionel train set. The thing really did work and we even had some sort of pill to put in the smoke stack that made it look like smoke was really comin' out of the train. Some fifty years later, Chip still has that train and puts it around his tree every Christmas. Some of those old Christmas trees were so scraggly I just can't hardly believe we would gawk at 'um all googie-eyed and make the same stupid comment every year: "That's the prettiest tree ever". Guess it's true that beauty is in the eyes of the beholder and us beholders were so wrapped up in what was goin' on we only saw what we wanted to see and not what was really there. Either that, or we weren't so picky in those days. Lookin' back on some of the black and white pictures we took with that ol' Brownie instamatic camera are hilarious. Made no difference back then, those trees were beautiful to us at the time and by crackie - that's all that mattered.

The bedroom that Chip and I shared was directly over the livin' room where the Christmas tree was. There was a hole in the floor 'long side the floor heater, where if you took the heater vent out you could see right down on the tree. Every Christmas Eve we always tried to catch Santa Claus but never did. Ol' Santa was either invisible or came by mighty late at night.

Us kids were early risers on Christmas mornin'. Mom and Dad always slept in a little, like they'd been up late the night before or somethin'. Never could get a grip on why they had to pick that one particular mornin' to sleep in. Specially, since, they made us go to bed early the night before. Seemed to me they shoulda' practiced their own preachin'. Anyway, they told us we weren't allowed to go downstairs without them. We'd be fussin' and carryin' on about them sleepin' in and not bein' up when they were supposed to be and Chip and I would be yellin' stuff like: "Hurry up, we can't wait no longer" or "This ain't fair, you all sleepin' in on Christmas mornin'" or "Come on hurry up". There were a few Christmas mornin's when Chip and I took the heater vent out so as to get a glimpse at what Santa had brought. Kinda' like a little preview of the toys if ya know what I mean. That usually made the anticipation even worse. Karen and Kevin weren't above lookin' through the vent either which made the delay even more unbearable yet 'cause then there was four of us gettin' after Mom and Dad.

When they did finally get up, they always had to go downstairs first and waste more valuable time. We were at the top of the stairs, chompin' at the bit to get the ball rollin' and finally permission was granted to come on down. We came down those stairs like four bowling balls - missin' about every other step, rounded the banister post and like Derby horses made a beeline for the tree. There was always somethin' special for each of us that would occupy time and slow the whole shootin' match down. The grand parents weren't always there on Christmas mornin', but, when they were that made it all the more fun. Within the hour the room was a pile of wrappin' paper, boxes and toys scattered everywhere. I always felt like Christmas is for kids and we were kids. Felt that way then and still do. Just can't find the words to describe how wonderful Christmas was at the farm.

Santa Claus always brought each of us kids one big present. That big present wasn't necessarily big in size – but it was somethin' special. One year a baseball glove, one year a bow and arrow, etc. That big present was the one thing we wanted more than anything in the whole wide world and each year Santa just somehow knew what it was and put it right there under the tree. The year when I was about eleven or so, there wasn't any big present for me. I wasn't disappointed about that – I was thankful for all the other stuff I had gotten. That particular year after all the presents had been opened and things started slowin' down a trifle, Mom and Dad suggested that we walk up to the Porter's house and wish them a Merry Christmas. I thought that was a pretty good idea myself, so off we went. About five minutes after we got there, Mr. Porter said he had to go get somethin' out of the other shed he had. That shed had a locked door, so with key in hand we were right behind him. When Mr. Porter opened the door I couldn't believe my eyes. Right there in front of me was a brand spankin' new "used" bicycle, handle bar tassels and all, with a sign on it that read: "Merry Christmas, Mike – Love Santa". Ol' Santa really hit the nail on the head that year!

That bicycle was my ticket to paradise. Now, instead of ridin' the horse across the same ol' fields and woods, I could go flyin' down the road anywhere I wanted to go. First thing I done was put a wire basket on it for pickin' up coke bottles 'long side the road. My coke bottle territory was now endless and I would soon be rich.

I gussied that thing up 'til Hell wouldn't have it. Soon as Spring rolled around and baseball season started, I put baseball cards on the front and rear tire supports with clothes pins and made myself a pretty real soundin' motor cycle. Used to ride that thing down to Bull Run to where the bridge went across the river into Prince William County and then on to Manassas. Didn't use to fish there much 'cause the walk was just too far - when I could cut through the woods and be to the Run a little further downstream in half the time. That bicycle gave me a whole new world. When I was in the sixth grade, Mom even let me ride it the three miles to school. Back then if you rode a bike to school you were considered cool. Reason was, most kids didn't have bicycles and even if they did, their parents still made them ride the bus.

Christmas vacation in the 50's was a real Christmas vacation. We got out of school around December the 20th and didn't have to go back 'til after new years. If you'd a gone to Clifton elementary back in those days, you'd have a rough idea how bad we needed that much time off. I'm sure the teachers were just tappin' their toe to get back, so as to continue our misery, but we sure as the devil weren't in any hurry.

We had many a White Christmas at the farm and with pert' near two weeks off, we did ourselves an awful lot of sleigh ridin'. My big present one year was a brand new, store bought "Flexible Flyer" sled. When I say brand new, that's just what I mean – brand new never been used! Jon had his own sled. He named it and painted right on it, "The Star Flight Jon". I figured my sled was better and faster than his so I named mine, "King Kong, Esq". It was medium in length and I probably could'a picked a better name - when considerin' how reliable, hard workin' and dependable that thing was. The "King Kong" part of the name was fine, it's the "Esq." part that was bein' a little hard on such a reliable contraption. And one more thing, King Kong never was an attorney but it was too late, I had already painted it on. There was a year or two we brought the Christmas tree home on that sled. Still have the ol' King Kong, Esq. and wouldn't part with it for love nor money.

Jon's farm had some mighty good hills for sleigh ridin'. The one facin' our house went straight down to a creek. If you didn't cut hard to the right you'd run flat-dab into either the creek bank or the barbed wire fence. We had it down just perfect and after a good many runs down the hill the sleigh run was slick as glass. I'd almost bet cha' we hit a hundred miles an hour on occasion.

Wasn't hardly any traffic on those old back country roads in those days and when it snowed there was next to none. They probably didn't have any more than three or four snowplows to cover all of Fairfax County and Clifton wasn't high on the priority list. Don't ever recall seein' a snowplow go past our house even in the summer time. That was the biggest plus we had and we didn't even realize it. There was a pretty steep hill across the way in front of the Pearson's house and after a few cars had eventually made it down the road, the snow was packed just right. At the top of the hill we'd build a fire right in the middle of the road. We sleigh rode there 'til well after midnight many a time. Somebody always brought a flashlight or two, but we didn't really need 'um. The hill was straight down and 'less you were a complete idiot there was no way you were goin' to run off the road even in the dark. After we got 'bout froze up solid, we'd call it a night and head on back across the road home. The house was a lot closer than was the bottom of the hill. Only problem was – once you finally made it back up the hill – the bottom was just too dog-gone invitin' and you wanted to haul butt down - just one more time – even after midnight. I'm goin' to tell ya one thing that's as true as the tooth fairy – leavin' that hill and the fire in the road was a mighty hard thing to do after we'd packed the snow down so perfect and that the road seemed so thankful for our efforts. Oh well, it would still be there in the mornin'.

Had another sleigh run down through the apple orchard behind the tool shed. There was a semi-steep grade with a sharp turn and a long straight away. At the end of the straight-away there was another little dip that went down a ways to the road. Once on the road and past the Lewis' house, there was one more grade all the way to the Fadley's driveway. I'd guess a hundred and fifty yards in all when conditions were right.

There was another dog at the farm and, because it was so many years ago, I just can't remember how we came about gettin' her. We named her Molly and she was a fine Irish Setter bitch. Molly was smarter than a text book and could run like the wind. Now that I was mobile with the new bicycle and all, she followed me everywhere I went. Sleigh ridin' was no exception. You probably ain't goin' to believe this part of the story, but it's true. When I had made me a good sleigh run down through the orchard, I'd start out up by the tool shed next to the driveway. I'd take off runnin' and jump on my sled belly first layin' down. If ya don't know much about sleigh ridin', that's how ya do it when you really want to go fast. Anyway, Molly would chase me for about thirty feet and then jump right on my back and ride down the hill. She liked the fast part of sleigh ridin' so when I started slowin' down, she'd jump off and look at me as though to say: "That sure was fun, let's do it again". Ol' Molly was mighty lovable, and a smart Irish girl, too.

Usually by late December most of the farm ponds and Bull Run had froze over. We weren't the best ice skaters in the world, but then, we weren't bad for our age. We never got no lessons on how to do stuff – we just figured it out for ourselves and did it. If Jon's mother, or even Ma for that matter, ever knew about ice skatin' on Bull Run, they'd a had a conniption. Us boys would take our skates and walk down to the bridge. We never bothered to check the ice to make sure it was thick enough to support us. We just figured it would be, due to how cold the weather was. We put on our skates, laced 'um up real good and headed up stream toward the Kincheloe farm. We would spend the better part of a day sometimes, skatin' on the Run. We all knew where the shallow water was from when the river was down in the summer due to drought. Didn't want to skate there though had to go out in the middle. The word "Macho" hadn't come along yet back then, but I think that's what it was or somethin' similar anyway.

There was several times when the sun was out and the temperature started warmin' up. We'd be out in the middle of the Run about a couple hundred feet from either bank and hear a long, slow crackin' of the ice sound. I only remember one time hearin' that noise that I ever high-tailed for shore. We didn't pay any attention to danger back then and we sure as heck didn't take any safety precautions either. Even an idiot would have taken a rope in case the ice broke through and somebody needed savin'. Not us.

Another fun thing to do was take the 22 rifles down to the Run when the river was froze over. We'd find us a mess of those brown beer bottles along the road that the litterbugs left for us, gather 'um up and slid them way out on the ice. We did some pretty fancy shootin' at targets that responded real good. When ya hit one of those cold bottles with a shot, they busted into a million pieces. We didn't have to worry about anybody complainin' or interferin' with our fun, after all, there wasn't nobody around to complain. That's another one of them things I don't reckon I'd try doin' today!

Took the Christmas tree down around the first week of January. Somehow, we always managed to bust a couple of the tree ornament balls in both the puttin' up and takin' down of the tree. Mom and Dad never got mad at us kids when that happened 'cause they did it themselves, now and again, and knew the bustin' was just part of the process and an accident most of the time. Must admit though – we were a lot more careful in the puttin' 'um up than the takin' 'um down part of the deal. Takin' down the tree was a bummer for two reasons. First, it meant Christmas vacation was over and second, it was a mess. We usually hauled the Christmas tree down the driveway and disposed of it across the street in the woods. Never could get all of the tinsel off, so it wasn't too hard to find the Christmas trees from years past. Christmas in the country - back in the good ol' days, was a real experience and 'less you lived out one or two of 'um, there's no way to explain or describe in words, how wonderful they were.

The Birds and Bees

Over the years we had about every kind of animal you could think of at the farm - everything from Charlie the Bull to gold fish.

One kind of animal I hadn't mentioned so far was the rabbits. We built us a free standin' rabbit hutch out along side the corncrib big enough to hold a good many rabbits. It was a cage built on two by four legs and the bottom of the cage was about three feet off the ground. Had two sides to it – one for the Momma rabbits and one for the Pappa rabbits. Always wondered why we didn't just let 'um snuggle up together 'specially in the winter. Later found out that if ya did that, they'd run ya over with baby rabbits. Mom did mix and match 'um up every now and then for a spell, so we did have plenty of baby rabbits. 'Bout the only full time job I ever remember Kevin havin' was to feed and water the rabbits and she did a halfway decent job of that as I recall. I say halfway decent for a reason. In time the hutch would get sorta' like the horses stall but instead of biscuits there were raisins. Kevin must have come up with a mighty good excuse for not havin' to do that part of the job. I remember many a time cleanin' those cages out. Cleanin' up flattened out rabbit raisins all matted together was about a nasty job and it stunk too.

Kevin claimed the rabbits were hers and nobody else seemed to give a hoot whose they were. Every now and then, we'd kill off a few for eatin'. When it got to the point where there was too many of 'um in the cage, that was our way of balancin' things off like Mother Nature does. The way we done that, was to hold um' up by the back legs and whack um' back of the neck real good with a hammer handle. That might sound a little barbaric, but the whack snapped their neck and killed um' instantly. Cleanin' a rabbit was about the same as cleanin' a squirrel – skin um' out, cut off the worthless parts, wash um' up and freezer pack um'.

The only other animal that belonged to Kevin was an old gray farm cat she named Gregory. We weren't too much into technicalities when we were kids, but when the cat had a littler of kittens one day, Kevin up and changed the cat's name to Gregory Ann.

Ma was the smartest woman I ever knew. Didn't give her a whole lot of credit in the smarts department back then, but in later years most everything she'd said or done made sense. She wanted us kids to learn about the life cycle and her technique was indirect. Ma never got any books out of the library or explained to us 'bout sex and birth, or livin' or dyin'. Ma always wanted us to see the life cycles - right there firsthand - and later put the puzzle together for ourselves. I'm gunna' tell ya what - Ma was a pistol and she knew it all. She never shied away from answerin' our questions but only answered 'um to the level of our need and not with a whole bunch of unnecessary trimmins'. I bet Ma would have been a good "Tight Rope" walker in a circus, due to the fact that she knew how to balance everything out just right.

Whenever any of the female animals on the farm came into heat, it just seemed the males knew about it right away. Remember me tellin' ya about when Charlie the Bull got hung up on the fence? Well, there's an example of what I'm talkin' about. Made no difference whether it was the dogs, the pigs, the horses or the cows. Mom never told us what was goin' on when she had us watch the process, she just made sure we were there watchin'. When the females got 'umselves in a motherly way, there was a real simple explanation of how the babies were in the mothers stomach and in time would be born and soon enough we'd have piglets, or pups, or calves or bunnies. I don't think any of us put two and two together just then, but later in life it all made sense.

When the givin' birth part came around, Ma tried to make sure we were there for that too. She couldn't always coordinate us bein' around with the animal givin' birth, but we were there for an awful lot of 'um. Maggie would have the little Irish pups and we'd count 'um comin' along one at a time. When I was real little I thought she was Poo Poo'n the pups, but after watchin' a cow or a horse once or twice, I realized that's not where they were comin' from. Still no detailed explanations from Mom.

The young would need nursin' at first and Ma wanted us to see how the Momma animals took to raisin' their young. Some would be over protective and it was best to watch from a distance. Some didn't seem to mind, but that all depended on the animal. In time the nursin' thing was over and it was time for the young animals to start bein' normal - or in other words, eatin' on their own - kinda' like us kids at the dinner table or thereabouts.

Now and again, one of the animals would be gettin' up in the years and about ready to cash out. Mom wanted us there for that too. She always thought the dyin' process, though sometimes sad, was as important as all the rest. In time we'd seen it all - and it was for us kids to figure out how the life cycle worked on our own.

Dad seldom seemed to be around when all this life cycle thing was goin' on and about the only thing I ever remember him tellin' me about any part of it - was when I was a little older. He'd say: "Don't bring nothin' home ya didn't leave with". I guess maybe that's the difference 'tween a Mom and a Dad. Moms seemed to be into the details and technicalities and Dads were only concerned with the overall picture.

Anyway ya shake it, Ma's outlook on life sure made a whole lot more sense than Dad's. Being a guy, I do understand Dad's approach and what he was gettin' at. Sorta' like Dad didn't mind buyin' the house if Ma didn't mind tendin' it. My mother's approach to teachin' her kids everything from the sex act to the grave sure made a lot of sense and challenged us kids to learn about life.

There was one other thing Ma taught us kids about life that really don't have much to do with what I'm talkin' about, but I want to tell ya about it anyway. It was about tellin' the truth and ownin' up for what ya done wrong. Ma baked a cake one day and somebody went and cut a slice out of it and ate it when she wasn't lookin'. Ma was pissed! When she asked us all who the guilty dog was – nobody fessed up. Ma made each one of us pull down our pants and bend over her knee. She spanked all four of our bare fannies real good. All's I can say 'bout that is – I done enough stuff to justify gettin' a good old fashioned spankin' now and again, but I never sliced that cake! Got a rough idea who done it, but I'll keep that to myself.

I only got one more thing to say about the life cycle thing - "Bout the time you *think* you've seen it all – try helpin' a cow or mare bear their young by pullin' while she's pushin' and then watch that little rascal stand up on those wobbly legs for the first time in life within a minute or so of birth. 'Til you've seen that –you ain't seen it all.

Horseback ridin' fields

Pumpkins growing in the corn field

Christmas tree 1953

Two mares with a colt

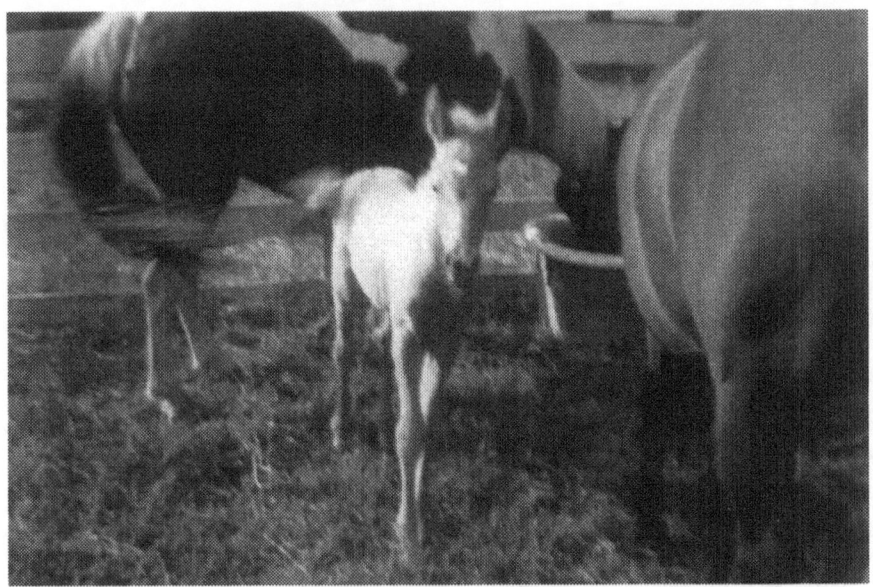

Me, Mom and Kevin with five little Duffy's

Abigail with her calf

"What's in a Name....."?

When livin' on a farm, it just seemed natural to have a name for everything. If somethin' didn't have a name, wasn't long before we took care of that. Sorta' like "Slow Poke Doak" for example. Once in a while, you'll hear some old-timer claim that lightnin' don't strike the same place twice – but that just ain't true. We had a giant Gum tree in the yard that got hit three times over the years and never once moved from where it was standin'. That was the "Pain in the Butt Tree" due to how much work it was rakin' up all them gumballs in the fall.

The tree across the way from it was what we called the "Indian Cigar Tree". It was actually a Catawba tree and I'm not sure how it came to be called the Indian Cigar Tree by us kids but that's what we called it. I already told ya about Pat's Hill and Fairyland and the names of all the cows, horses and dogs, so I want to move on to people.

Kevin's nickname was Vinegar. Probably not too hard to figure how us kids came up with Vinegar from the "Vin" in Kevin. She never paid much attention to us callin' her that, but I'll guarantee you one thing - if she'd of ever showed even one iota of dislike to it, we'd a poured it on.

I used to call Chip, "Chimp". I think I was the originator of that one and, to my best recollection, I'm the only one that ever called him that. I pretty much only used that flatterin' name when he'd done pissed me off about somethin'.

As for Karen, she got the nickname Ka Ka early in life. I never inquired as to how it came about, but it most likely came along from when Kevin and Chip were learnin' how to talk and that's how they pronounced Karen. She took a fancy to that name and always liked it. Many in the family still call her that.

As for me, my nickname was "Turtle Head". From the lookin' at angle, I never had no physical traits or any resemblance to a turtle, so let me tell ya where that one came from. I was just crazy 'bout those ol' box turtles that ya see crossin' the road every now and then. Back in the old days ya used to see 'um all the time, 'specially after a good ol' gully washer of a thunderstorm. No matter where we went, Mom would always stop so I could run back and get the turtle crossin' the road and take 'um home with me. We had a place out back of the house where Mom and Dad were plannin' to put on a small addition on to the house, but never got past diggin' the footin's. The area as best I can recall was 'bout 12 feet by 12 feet and the footin's were about a foot deep and a foot wide and the perfect place to keep the turtles. If they tried to get away, they dropped down in the shallow hole and I'd get 'um out the next day. I called the place "Turtle Island" and there was never less than of a mess of 'um on the island all summer long.

Now a'days, they're not around as much due to the modern highways and fast cars. The poor little guys don't have much of a chance crossin' the road anymore. I still stop for every one I see and get him out of the road. Don't take 'um home anymore, I just get 'um safely across the road to wherever they're headin' and go on. Makes me feel good for some reason or other.

One day when Chip and I were walkin' back home from Marshall and Nelly's, a turtle was crossin' the road just sorta' mindin' his own business. I think the devil took hold of Chip for a minute – no other logical explanation for what he done. The boy picked up a stick and smashed the poor thing's shell. That turtle was just about a mess with a busted shell and blood everywhere, but he was still alive. I picked the turtle up real gentle like and carried him home. Soon as I got there, I found me some mercurochrome and bandages and went into what ya might call some heavy duty country boy surgery. I shaped the shell back together and bandaged it up with Ma's adhesive tape. I tended and nursed that thing for the longest time. The shell eventually bonded like a broken bone and by summers end, he was good as new.

Another year I got me a can of yellow paint and every time I let one go back into the wild, I'd put a big yellow spot on the top of the shell. I guess ya might call that an early form of wildlife management or somethin'. Sure was cool to find an old friend for the second time. Always asked 'um where they'd been – but never got an answer.

The farmhouse across the way belonged to the Pearson's. The first couple of years after we moved to the farm, the house was rented out to some people named James. The two little girls had a younger brother named Butchie, who was about a year younger than me. Butchie was always gettin' in trouble and we didn't mind, even a little bit, helpin' him along with that. Butchie was the kind of kid who would do anything ya told him to do. If we told him to sit in a mud puddle, he'd do it. If we told him to pee in his pants, he'd do it. None of his doin's set well with his parents and he was always in dutch. Butchie had a nickname. We called him "Somboom" 'cause that was about the only word in his limited vocabulary. We later found out that his father went around callin' everything and everybody a Son-of-a-........ and Somboom was Butchie's little boy impersonation of his Dad.

Chip and I shared a small bedroom at the farm and for years we'd go to sleep every night by tellin' "Butchie Stories". Since Butchie would do anything ya told him to do, we just made up the stories every night about the wildest things we could imagine Butchie doin'. Chip would tell me one - then I'd tell him one. That went on 'til we dozed off. Butchie stories were told every night for a long, long time. A few years back, Chip and I went to Atlantic City for the night and shared a motel room. After we turned the lights out, I said: "Hey Chip, I want to tell you a 'Butchie story". We both had a good laugh then dozed off.

Originality, damn sure ain't no trait of country folks. When Butchie and them moved off somewhere else, one of the Pearson sons moved off the lower farm into the house. His name was Raymond Edgar Pearson, Sr. so naturally his oldest son was named Raymond Edgar Pearson, Jr. Raymond, Jr. liked to do a lot of showin'-off, whenever he took a notion. Country folk called showin'-off, "Peartin'". Didn't take long before ol' Raymond Jr. done picked up the nickname, "Peart Pearson". In time that was shortened to just plain ol' "Peart". His younger sister, Delores, was my age and we even started the first grade together. She was a nice girl and a little refined when compared to the rest of 'um. Her nickname was "Piggy". She was a slim girl and I think the name came from when her job was sloppin' the hogs down on the lower farm before she moved up topside. Nobody but her own family ever called her that God-awful name and, fortunately for her, it never stuck at school. About six years after Delores, along came another boy. The Dad done used up the name Raymond Edgar on the first one, so he decided to name the younger boy Edgar Raymond.

Chip always thought that name thing was hilarious. Any time you'd ever refer to either boy in any way, he'd say: "Wait a minute now, are you talkin' about Raymond Edgar or Edgar Raymond?" and laugh like a hyena. I thought it was right funny myself and used to say the same thing all the time.

People down the road were named Jasper. They lived on a farm and were good friends of Uncle Moir and Aunt Gen. Don't know that they actually were - but you'd of thought they were some kin to the Pearson's - when it came to divvyin' up names. The old mans name was Jones Jasper. And, if that ain't country, I don't know what is. That was another one Chip had fun with. The boy had a pretty simple sense of humor, back in them days. He'd say: "Now hold on, is his name Jones Jasper or Jasper Jones?". Anyway, there were three boys in the family, John, Jonathan and J.J.

Even though J.J. was around my age, I never did get around to askin' him what the initials stood for. Bet ya two bits if I had'a - it would have been some concoction of the other two.

The Burton family lived less than a half a mile up the road. The oldest boy was named Junior. To the best of my recollection, that was his real first name and not a nickname for bein' the first kid down the family line. Junior never seemed to go to school, so I'm not real sure what the story was on him. The younger son Billy was my age. He was a pretty cool guy and we used to call him Billy Burpton.

When ya got as far away from the farm as Clifton, there was a guy named "Tilt" Mathers and another named ""Buzzard" Burke. Additionally, there was "Swim" Elgin, "Taffy" Hall, "Harvey Toons" Mathers and "Tiny" Burke. Tiny got his nick name 'cause he was so big. Gotta' admit one thing - those names were "Hum Dingers". Never knew where them first names came from and I ain't rightly sure I'd want any of 'um for myself. Dad always called Donna Tolson "Bambi". That one was kinda cute, I always thought, and so was she.

My friends, it's time to ask you a question. Understandin' one thing now - these names and nicknames were all real and within a mile or so, as the crow flies, from the farmhouse (With the exception of the Cliftoners). But what's really in a name? I think it was either Charlie Brown or Snoopy who once said: "A rose by any other name would smell just as good". That said - all these good people, places, things and animals were just as good no matter what ya called 'um. Sometimes I think our old mule, Jake the Flake, whose only claim to fame was eatin' lit cigarettes right out of Grandma Anna's mouth - was the only one who didn't give a flip about anything – and he had a name everybody laughed at. What difference did it make anyway? None! – He didn't give a hoot and his name wasn't gunna' change – it was still "Jake the Flake" anyway ya shake it - and we loved him even if he was a jackass.

Butchie left - Me right with the redbone pups

Me and "Jake the Flake"

Us kids just hangin' out

Grandma's House

Even though the farm was a fun place to be, sometimes it was just down-right nice to get away. Grandma Lawrence had a house in Bay Ridge, Maryland and 'most every summer we'd go there for a spell on vacation.

Winters on the farm were brutal with two foot snow storms and winds that drifted the snow five and six feet across the road, or anywhere there was an embankment where the wind could blow it.

It wasn't uncommon for the power lines to break and leave us stranded like rats on a sinkin' ship. Most of the neighbors had outhouses, no indoor runnin' water and used wood stoves in the winter for heat. Long as they could blaze a trail to the quarter moon door, they didn't give a hoot whether the power lines were up or down. We were different. We'd kinda' got used to the ol' porcelain convenience, runnin' water and indoor heat. Campin' out in the kitchen in front of the gas stove all day and wearin' winter coats to bed was new to us. We were lucky though – we were the "Upper Crust", by comparison, and unlike some, we did have a "Pot to Pee in" and I mean that literally. Another of my nasty jobs was emptyin' that thing. There were times when that lifestyle dragged on for a week or better.

When summer rolled around we went to Grandma's on vacation for a week or two. Bay Ridge, Maryland was a suburb of Annapolis and right on the Chesapeake Bay. Bay Ridge was an old community even back in the 50's and most residents lived in that quiet little place year 'round. If you moseyed on down to the point you could see across Spa Creek to downtown Annapolis. Up the street from Grandma's about three houses or so was a house that sat back off the road a right good ways. The people who lived there must have had 15 or 20 purple martin birdhouses on poles. The houses were all different and attracted hundreds of martins. Visiting their lane in the evenin's after dinner was almost as big a thrill as when the Good Humor ice cream truck came along about the same time of day. We'd never seen a Good Humor Man before and he apparently didn't know where Clifton, Virginia was either so understandably, we'd never made his acquaintance nor him ours. When he came down the street – the sound of that Good Humor bell was somethin' I'll just never forget. Kinda' like hearin' a grouse drummin' or a West Virginia bobcat screamin' in the night – you just never forget it. Anytime Mom and Dad had enough extra money for a real treat, we kids were headin' for that truck in fourth gear. There's somethin' about the Good Humor man that lasts forever in the memories of yesteryear.

Only thing we ever had out at the farm with any degree of resemblance to the Good Humor man was the Milk Man, who came around about once a week. We looked forward to his comin' around too and I'll tell ya why. We'd beg him for an ice cube like a hound dog beggin' for a bone. He was always accommodatin' and that was a big deal to us. Those ice cubes were a real luxury and somethin' special on a hot summer day.

At the end of the street and around the bend was a community meetin' hall with a dock, boats and all. Mom and Dad always timed our vacation to Grandma's house with the annual Bay Ridge Jamboree. Most people walked to the Jamboree so there was never any traffic jams or parkin' problems. When ya live on a farm and then visit the big city, 'bout anything you see is impressive. That Jamboree was a Barnum & Bailey Circus to us. They didn't have any lions and tigers there – didn't even have any elephants or high wire acts. What they did have was a half a dozen little rides, and some games like pick a plastic duck out of the revolvin' water tank and if it had the right number on the bottom, you won a prize.

Slot machines were legal in Maryland in the 50's and there were a bunch of those there too. That Jamboree sure was fun.

There was a swimmin' area just below the house with jetties goin' out in the water about 60 feet and sandy beaches. There was water as far as the eye could see and gentle waves rollin' right onto the beach. Since none of us kids had ever seen anything more than Bull Run or a farm pond, this was Atlantic City as far as we were concerned.

Grandma didn't live there full time and when we showed up the small lawn always needed mowin' and the bushes needed trimmin' - just the kinda' stuff we were tryin' to get away from. She had one of those ol' wooden stick handled lawn mowers where the blades only turned when ya pushed it. We couldn't help but notice that those things worked a whole lot better when the grass was short - on account of we had to mow it again before we left. Ma told us boys to get to work and within a couple of hours, we had the place lookin' lived in.

By the time we were old enough and had a little responsibility to us, Ma let us swim in the Chesapeake Bay on our own, unchaperoned, and we even had store bought bathin' suits this time around. That was just great for two reasons. First, when we were little, times were tough and if memory serves me correctly, our introduction to the Chesapeake Bay was in our Fruit of the Looms and second, now that we were all grown up we were doin' things like normal people. Grandma always had a couple of those old inner tubes for car tires layin' around, so all we had to do was pump 'um up with one of those bicycle tire pumps and we were in business – floatin' in the Bay. If that wasn't a country boy's "Paradise", I need somebody to tell me what was. Every single year we seemed to always manage to time our vacation with when the sea nettles peaked out. Gettin' stung by one of those things wasn't quite as bad as a hornet, but it did sure as heck get your attention. Some kid told us one year to rub sand on the sting and it would quit hurtin'. That might sound like an "Old Wives Tale" but it really did work, for the most part. Pickin' 'tween the remedy or not gettin' stung in the first place - didn't take us long to figure it was all around better just not gettin' stung.

Grandma had a crab net and an old galvanized bucket out in the shed behind the house. So naturally, I took up crabbin' when other entertainment started runnin' low. A crab net is just that, a net on the end of a wooden handle. The jetties extended a right good ways out into the water and were put in to keep the sandy beach from erodin' durin' storms. They consisted of a wooden wall supported by posts driven way down in the ground under the water. The center wall had 6 by 6 wooden supports attached horizontally above the water line even durin' high tide. The general construction made them perfect for walkin' out on all the way to the end. In the early mornin' or late afternoon when the tides had already changed and the water was calm, the ol' crabs used to love to cling on to them in a lazy sort of way, just takin' it easy out of harms way – or so they thought.

One year, when I was around 9 or 10 years old, I made me a live-box for puttin' 'um in. Made that thing at the farm and carried it all the way to Grandmas house for usin'. It was a rectangular box made out of 2 by 4's and lath strips with a hinged door on it for dumpin' the crabs in then closing back up. Hooked a rope to it where I could tie it to the end of a jetty for keepin' the crabs in 'til I had enough of them to sell to Dad.

I walked them jetties every day. I'd take a couple of steps at a time lookin' on both the right side and then the left 'til I spied one there just hangin' out, mindin' his own business. As soon as I saw one, his business became my business and I'd ease the net down in the water and grab him in the net, put him in the bucket and head out for another one. When I'd got me a mess of 'um, I'd sell the jumbos to Dad for a dollar a dozen. A dollar a dozen might not sound like a lot of money but it was to me back then, considerin' it would take me a week or better to make as much at home rakin' leaves and haulin' them to the compost pile at 2 cents a gunny sack full. Or you could look at it from a different angle – that equated to 50 coke bottles at 2 cents each and that would have taken me months or even longer to do. Grand Daddy helped defer the total expense by pitchin' in 50 cents of the dollar so as not to make it too rough on Dad, but then he ate half the crabs - so I guess his kindness wasn't all for naught. Long and short of the whole deal was, everybody, but the crabs, was happy includin' me, and I was gettin' rich.

When we were real little, Dad used to take us kids up to the point to do some fishin'. Dad had a regular rod and reel, but us kids had to use a homemade hand line fishin' get up. A hand line wasn't anything more than a small piece of wood with fishin' string wound around it with a hook and a sinker on the end.

We did catch some fish every now and then – but at best, it was exactly like I just said – every now and then. Chip and I used to do some night fishin' off the end of the jetty closest to Grandma's house. We never caught anything worth braggin' about – mostly blowfish or a slimy ol' eel once in a while.

One year, Grandma had come by a sailboat. We never asked her where she got it, but one thing was for sure – it wasn't one for no heavy-duty sailin'. The thing was around 10 feet long and made out of Styrofoam with a plastic sail. Chip and I decided one mornin' to do some sailin' - even though neither one of us had ever been on a sailboat. We didn't need no sailin' lessons - we knew what we were doin'. Didn't need any of those fancy gadgets like oars or life vests either. We hoisted the sail, got in and we were sailin'. Everything was goin' as planned 'til we got out past the ends of the jetties and the wind started takin' us up the Bay and out further and further. "Bout the time we'd gotten out pretty doggone far, I figured it was time to ask Chip what he reckoned we ought to do. Chip told me in a less than reassurin' voice: "Don't worry, I know what I'm doin'". I was tellin' ya a while ago about country boy ingenuity - well, Chip was usin' a little common sense and a whole lot of luck when he navigated that thing against the wind. Somehow, he got us safely back to where we'd started out. I don't believe either of us has ever been on a sailboat since.

The car ride to Bay Ridge seemed to take forever with seven people, countin' Duffy, and all our stuff in one car. Duffy wasn't a kennel kind of dog, so where we went – he went. It really wasn't all that far mileswise, but, back then there wasn't any beltway or air conditionin' in the car, and the anticipation of gettin' there made the ride seem twice as long. When we were headin' down the last stretch, way before you could even see the Chesapeake Bay, Duffy would start sniffin' in so hard it sounded like he had a cold or somethin'. Ol' Duffy could smell the Bay water from a half a mile or better and he knew what was ahead. Duffy liked goin' to the beach as much as we did and we never had to coax him in the water for a swim.

The ride home after our vacation seemed even longer than gettin' there. None of us wanted to leave so much fun, 'specially with the though of school startin' back up in a week or so. Those family vacations to Bay Ridge were like a trip to "Wonderland".

Grandmas house - Bay Ridge, Maryland
Karen, Chip, Me and Kevin

Bay Ridge - Mom, Dad, Grandma and Grandpa
with me in the middle - summer 1951

Chip Bay Ridge
1958
(Jetty in back)

Bay Ridge, Maryland - around 1950
Fishing trip to the point - Dad, Me, Karen & Duffy, Kevin & Chip.

Karen center, Kevin, Me and Chip.

Me at the beach with Jetty in the background.

Yours truly!

It's All Over But The Cryin'.....

I had me a pet squirrel one time that fell out of a tree one night durin' a thunderstorm. I was out walkin' around the next mornin' and all but stepped on the little rascal. He wasn't any bigger than a pipsqueak and appeared hurt real bad. When I picked him up off the ground, he was sorta' favorin' one back leg. Common sense would tell ya that he broke the leg and that's why he was layin' there on the ground in the first place. I fed him some milk with an eyedropper and brought him back around 'til I could get him to the Veterinarian. The Vet told me the leg wasn't broke, but he'd hurt it plenty bad in the fallin' out of the tree. I kept him around - and pretty much took up where his mother left off in the raisin' process. Named the squirrel Darby.

I took ol' Darby 'bout everywhere I went and most of the time he'd just sit on my shoulder 'til he suspected trouble then he'd run down my shirt, slip through between the button holes and nestle up in the lower inside where I had the shirt tucked into my pants. After he was grown I fed him candy kisses and chunks of sweet potato. 'Most any time he was pesterin' me, like when eatin' at the dinner table or somethin', I'd put a candy kiss in his mouth and he'd run up the drapes to the top and set there 'til he was done. The boy wasn't too much on sharin' food. Darby was the laziest squirrel Mother Nature had ever come up with. Many a mornin' I had to shake him pretty good to even wake him up.

After about a year and a half, Darby started changin' - kinda like a kid does when he hits teenage. Started gettin' a little independent and feisty - he even nipped me a couple of times for no particular reason. Wasn't like the Devil got to him or anything like that - I knew what was goin' on – 'cause it had happened to me a time or two - ol' Darby had either seen or smelled a girl squirrel and the call of the wild done got a hol't to him. I knew I had to let him go off on his own – lettin' him figure out what to do when he got there. Took him out back one day, put a candy kiss in his mouth and stuck him on the side of a tree. He did just what I knew he'd do – he ran up the tree to the first branch and was out of sight. I wished him well and walked away. Never laid eyes on the boy again.

Only reason I tell ya the story 'bout Darby was due to the same thing happenin' to all of us kids. Kids and squirrels have a little somethin' in common when hittin' a certain age. Can't put all the blame on us kids though, Mom's and Dad's change a little too. Dad had bought him a Ford Dealership all the way over in Upper Marlboro, Maryland and due to the distance, 'bout the only time we ever saw him was on weekends. Ma said, Dad spent many a night sleepin' in his office in his chair with his desk for a pillow. Dad needed to move closer to where he was workin' and us kids were on to that idea like a cat on a mouse.

When a young boy gets to the point where he starts payin' attention to the girls as *attractions* rather than *distractions*, it's time to ease up on the farm boy life style of life and start concentratin' on more manly things. I was ready to move to the big city and as far as I was concerned – the farm could stay right there in the boon-docks and get along just fine without me. It was 'long about mid June of 1963 when a movin' company called, "Craig Movers" from Oakton, Virginia showed up one mornin' to save the day and change my life from a pitiful ol' country boy to one of respectability.

I was 15 when we moved off the farm and into a brand spankin' new house in a subdivision called "Rutherford" off Guinea Road in Fairfax, Virginia. Took considerable time to learn the new life style of city livin'. Chip and I were fast learners though and picked up on most things 'bout as quick as which way to run when the bees were gettin' after ya. The new house had what was called central air conditionin'. I'd never seen or even heard of air conditionin' and had no idea how it worked. One thing was for sure though, it beat the heck out of leavin' the windows open at the farmhouse on a hot summer's day or night. I remember one particular night at the farm when I was layin' in bed swelterin' - and sweatin' like a pitcher of Koolaid. To make bad matters worse, there was an ol' hoot owl in the oak tree 'long side the tool shed. Like'ta never dozed off that night. The air conditioner had a hum to it that put ya to sleep faster than a lullaby. This was livin'. The house even had a slidin' glass door downstairs for goin' outside. I'll never forget my introduction to the door – walked smack-dab, face first into it, thinkin' there wasn't anything there. I was mighty glad nobody saw me do it - and right now is the first and only time I ever told anybody 'bout doin' that.

Opportunity seemed endless in the big city. Now, instead of ridin' my bike for miles pickin' up coke bottles for 2 cents each or rakin' leaves, I could mow lawns in the neighborhood. Used to mow the inside lots for a dollar fifty and the corner lots for two bucks. Gettin' to the next job on foot and usin' my own lawn mower and gas weren't even factors in my gettin' rich quick game plan – the profit was just too high. Comin' off the farm, I couldn't believe people were that rich or that lazy to pay some kid to mow their lawn - and a dollar fifty on top of that!

My best friend Dorian Fullerton, was the first of my Clifton friends to get his driver's license and he didn't mind drivin' to Fairfax any more than I minded livin' there. He had one of those old black Volks Wagon beetles with a four speed on the floor and an AM radio. What more could we possibly need or ask for? That old VW was our "Free Pass" to Heaven on earth. Gas was still around 25 cents a gallon and the VW got 40 miles to the gallon. We rode "Forever" on a dollar's worth. Bein's I was gettin' a dollar fifty for a regular lawn mowin' job, that equated to "Forever and a Half's" worth of ridin'. I was in "Hog Heaven" – or so I thought.

I never gave the farm too much thought durin' the mid to late 60's on account I was too busy in high school playin' sports and messin' with the girls - and they were everywhere. Always hoped my geography teacher would ask us on a test to define "Natural Resources" but she never did. There wasn't much else in my life at that time other than sports, girls and good times.

I had an occasion to return to Clifton several years ago. It took me better than 30 years to return and face the reality of the times. If you ever saw the movie, "Valley of the Dolls", than you know what *"real"* going home is all about. Most people, somehow, never really know how much they miss something until they miss it really bad. Some people have a tendency to forget how wonderful something was – until it isn't there any more and never will be again – that's what I'm really trying to say. That particular day the bright lights of the big city seemed to fade faster than swatting a fly. All the things - which weren't there anymore, came back like a bad dream – or good dream – all depending on perspective.

I felt helplessly pitiful and embarrassed that I had been in such a hurry to get away from the farm. That farm hadn't been anything but good to me and I couldn't get away from it fast enough. The farm had given me a good life that I never even saw while living it. Mr. Porter once told me: "The day will come when you won't need me anymore - you'll have a wife and family of your own". Like everything else he ever said, that made sense to me at the time. I just, somehow, couldn't buy it that day. I needed him right then and right there. I needed him that day serving as the same security blanket he did as a child – but he wasn't there. How humbling I felt standing there thinking – *knowing* - I never even took the time to say good-bye to Mr. Porter, the man who took me in, as the son he never had - the man who taught me how to find

Indian arrowheads and how to identify trees by their bark or leaves – and now he was gone – *forever*. Another emptiness came crashing down like a loose bale of hay from the loft. I had left the shillelagh of the great Shaunus O'Murphy in the tool shed, so many years ago. Once my most prized possession in the whole world - and I left it in the tool shed in my haste to get away. I'd swap anything I own to have that thing today – I'd even get a bank loan if necessary. Humiliation started settling in when I thought about being in such a hurry to get away - that I hadn't even said good-bye to any of my other good friends either - the cows, the horses or even the frogs down at the creek who were kind enough to give me their tadpoles every year to take to school. I hadn't even taken the time for one final walk to the dump or through the house or the barn and it was way too late now for any "I'm Sorry's" or "Good-Byes". Mr. Porter told me on several occasions: "You need to slow down long enough to smell the roses". I don't much recall ever taking heed - or the time - to do that - and now, everything had changed - except the memories.

The farm – that blessing of my youth - that Mom and Dad provided us kids with as children was sold and divided into five-acre estates. The house had not changed at all - still standing majestically with the strength of a plow horse and the grace and splendor of a bearded iris. The fields where we used to grow corn and dove hunt every September and the fields where we used to ride the horses were now estates with homes and lawns. And where the corn shucks once stood and the pumpkins once grew, sat a Mercedes or BMW. The road to the dump had been widened and paved and it was difficult to even determine where I was while driving along. Under those lawns and pavement lay all of the Indian arrowheads we hadn't found yet. With a tear in my eye and a lump in my throat - Tara from "Gone with the Wind" seemed more of a reality than just a house and a farm in a movie.

Clifton proper hadn't changed too much either. The old hotel had been renovated and was operational. The Buckley's Store, which had been boarded up and vacant just about the whole time we were there, was now a restaurant and they'd added on to Clifton Elementary and made it a little bigger. Other than that, the magnolia tree was still in Mrs. Buckley's front yard, the streetlights were still the same, the train track was just as we had left it – and that "Cute as a Gnats Eyelash" little ol' country town hadn't changed a wink. It's a crying shame some people don't realize what they had - until they no longer have it. I guess you'd say, I learned a lesson the hard way, perhaps the sad way…. Clifton, Virginia is still in my heart – and like the red head on a woodpecker – that ain't gunna' change – And - I don't want it to either.